SHAKING A FIST
AT GOD

SHAKING A FIST AT GOD

Struggling with the Mystery
of Undeserved Suffering

Katharine Dell

TRIUMPH™ BOOKS
Liguori, Missouri

Published by Triumph™ Books
Liguori, Missouri
An imprint of Liguori Publications

Library of Congress Cataloging-in-Publication Data

Dell, Katharine J. (Katharine Julia), 1961–
    Shaking a fist at God : struggling with the mystery of undeserved
suffering / Katharine Dell. — 1st U.S. ed.
        p.   cm.
    Originally published : London : Fount Paperbacks, 1995.
    Includes bibliographical references.
    ISBN 0-7648-0030-2
    1. Bible. O.T. Job — Criticism, interpretation, etc. 2. Suffering —
Religious aspects — Christianity. I. Title.
BS1415.2.D45   1997
223'.106 — dc20   96-26517

Katharine Dell asserts the moral right to be identified as the author of this work.
Originally published in English by Fount, an imprint of HarperCollins Publishers Ltd under the title *Shaking a Fist at God*

01 00 99 98 97 5 4 3 2 1
Printed in the United States of America
First U.S. Edition

In memory of Christine

Contents

Foreword

I am dedicating this book to the memory of a good friend. We each have some story of suffering to tell, and I suppose this is one that is common enough and yet it happens to be mine.

It wasn't as if I really needed another friend—I already had a best friend and at the age of twelve one is usually enough. But a girl sat near to me and used to make me laugh with her dancing brown eyes and friendly smile. She was always the one in the class to do something unusual—she never followed fashion, she created her own and scoured the second-hand clothes shops for an outfit that hadn't been seen since the twenties. She loved to surprise people—like the day when she came into class with all her flowing locks shorn into the shortest haircut you could imagine. She loved the reaction it brought out in people. She and I were both dreamers—I think that is what we had in common. We used to dream about the future—about the time when we would be out of this prison called school and we would be making our way in the world. We would meet ideal partners, we would become successes—all the dreams teenage girls have. She dreamt herself into various different careers. She wanted at one time to be an artist—she had a certain flair—and we spent time writing a children's book together—I writing the story and she providing the illustrations.

She went on to do the kind of things many people do, I suppose—going to university and getting a good job, although she never lost that originality and freshness, that daring and sense of the fun in life. We met infrequently latterly and yet whenever we did meet or speak on the telephone the old repartee always came back straight away. It is often said of an old friend that you can just pick up where you left off. I think there was a strong understanding of each other as well as a strong affection.

Well, the tragic tale is that at the age of 26 she was killed falling off the back of a motorbike. It happened in a few seconds. She had scarcely ridden one before but it was entirely in keeping with her sense of adventure that she should give it a try. She had written to me only a few weeks before it happened telling me that she was thinking of taking up flying. She also told me in this letter that now she had moved to London she was having a marvellous time, and she wrote 'I feel as if life is just beginning for me'. The irony of that remark stayed with me for a long time after her death. I suppose the suffering was for all those who knew her and loved her. My hope is that she didn't herself suffer too much. Her mother telephoned and told me the news, and I was so shocked I could hardly say anything. I have often thought of all the things I wanted to say at that moment and couldn't. Whilst the suffering for her family must have been much worse than for me, a mere school friend, I was deeply affected. Something died within me too at that moment, something of the laughter and the joy, something of the dreams and hopes. There was she, a person so full of life, who had lost her life. It all seemed so unfair.

This book is an attempt to explore the problem of undeserved suffering and the protest that we often want to make. It is dedicated to her in memory of a good friendship and of those sadly curtailed hopes and dreams.

SHAKING A FIST
AT GOD

1

Our Common Experience

Her experience had been of a kind to teach her, rightly or wrongly, that the doubtful honour of a brief transit through a sorry world hardly called for effusiveness, even when the path was suddenly irradiated at some halfway point by daybeams rich as hers. But her strong sense that neither she nor any human being deserved less than was given, did not blind her to the fact that there were others receiving less who had deserved much more. And in being forced to class herself among the fortunate she did not cease to wonder at the persistence of the unforeseen, when the one to whom such unbroken tranquillity had been accorded in the adult stage was she whose youth had seemed to teach that happiness was but the occasional episode in a general drama of pain.

Thomas Hardy,
The Mayor of Casterbridge

Each and every human being in every age has a story of suffering to tell. It may be the kind of suffering that we all experience at one time or another such as bereavement or estranged relationships. Or it may be on a larger scale—destruction of a lifelong home through natural disaster, victimization, the premature death of a close friend or relative through illness or accident. Every day we hear a different tale of suffering on the news—we are all very much aware of the suffering, both of individuals and of larger groups and nations. I suppose one has to admit that suffering is an inevitable part of human existence. But a large part of the nature of suffering is how we react to it. Some people take it badly, others find it easier to assimilate and cope with. Some let it drag them down into a cynical scepticism about life. I am reminded of the words of Hardy quoted at the beginning of this chapter. They come at the end of the book and describe Elizabeth-Jane, Henchard's daughter. The idea that happiness 'was but the occasional episode in a general drama of pain' is the experience of many who are not as lucky as Elizabeth-Jane, who in adult life finds happiness in marriage, social status and relative prosperity—what Hardy describes as 'a latitude of calm weather'. These words, however, express Hardy's own cynicism, resignation even, over whether life has any pattern or meaning. What comes over strongly in this passage is the idea that somehow there is a sys-

? I'm not so sure.

tem of 'just deserts' at work in life: '…her strong sense that neither she nor any human being deserved less than was given, did not blind her to the fact that there were others receiving less who had deserved much more'. Elizabeth-Jane shows a humility at not expecting too much out of life, and yet there is a sense that one deserves something although many people don't get what they deserve.

This is a common human reaction to suffering. We have a feeling that somehow life should be 'fair'. A certain amount of suffering we can cope with as a part of human existence, but when the suffering seems to be incongruous with the happiness we start to ask why. We sometimes feel bad about having done a particular thing, and then something else seems to come along to rectify the balance. We almost feel that we have deserved a little misfortune. This is also a common reaction— seeing a pattern in events—like the old adage that 'misfortunes happen in threes'. But when this balance is at all tilted in our minds it tends to be in the direction of hoping for prosperity. We seem to have an unspoken belief in goodness, in things working out, in disasters not happening daily and not to us. Despite suffering in the world there is still a great feeling of looking forward which somehow gets us through the suffering, a feeling of hope, a feeling of new life in the midst of death. However I have heard it said by some that they feel their life has been too easy—they have not had their fair share of suffering. The path of suffering is even sometimes seen as a higher calling—only through suffering can you really know yourself or most effectively help others.

In this book I want to ask why we react to suffering in these kinds of ways. Why, for example, do we have a limit on how much suffering we can cope with? Why do we have an unspoken expectation that life will 'work out for the best' somehow, and why furthermore do we always try to find someone to blame? When things go wrong we usually look to blame others—friends and loved ones even—sometimes we try to blame God. We rarely blame ourselves, or if we do, it is after much blaming of others—even the cat—to start with. If we try to blame God, why do we do so, what do we expect from him—where does he fit in?

Suffering is usually the issue on which most people find religion stumbles. How can you or I believe in a God who allows such suffering in the world? Dostoyevsky in *The Brothers Karamazov* raises this issue in a dramatic way. He has one of his characters, Ivan, insisting on the impossibility of believing in a God who lets a five-year-old child suffer innocently at the hands of parents who hate her:

> They beat her, birched her, kicked her, without themselves knowing why, till her body was covered with bruises....Do you realize what it means when a little creature like that, who's quite unable to understand what is happening to her, beats her little aching chest in that vile place, in the dark and cold, with her tiny fist and weeps searing, unresentful and gentle tears to 'dear, kind God' to protect her?

Ivan cannot imagine a God who would be the architect of a world in which this was allowed to happen. He finds it too much of God to ask of human beings: 'We cannot afford to pay so much for admission, and therefore I hasten to return my ticket of admission,' he says. Alyosha's answer is to point to the crucifixion and to Christ's power of forgiveness. We might draw parallels with what we often hear today of parent-child relationships that have gone drastically wrong. Richard Harries, in an

article called 'Evidence for the love of God', begins with a poi-
gnant example of innocent suffering on a par with Dostoyevsky's:

> 'Don't kill me, Mum.' These were the last words of an
> eight-year-old boy as his mother pushed him under the
> water in the bath and drowned him. Some years before
> this she had killed her two young babies but it was
> thought, mistakenly, that she was now in her right mind
> and her older boy was safe. Such incidents which, alas,
> we can read about every day, rock any religious faith we
> might have to the foundation. How on earth can there be
> a God of love behind a universe in which such appalling
> things happen?

Behind the question 'Why suffering?' is clearly the further question, 'How can we believe in a God who allows such suffering
to happen?' Phrasing such questions is natural enough but often springs from a misunderstanding of what 'religion' is. It is
not about easy answers or about religious people having a hot-
line to prosperity. It involves grappling with difficult questions
and not necessarily finding any rational answers. We might ask
if it is realistic to expect to find a reason for suffering. Furthermore, is it fair to blame God for the misfortunes that come
upon us? More helpful than asking unanswerable questions
such as 'Why suffering?' is, I suggest, trying instead to understand why we react in this way, and this is what I am trying to
do in this book. It may be that some religious outlooks have
fostered the misconception that there are simple answers to be
found. Since long ago 'wise men' have believed that good
behaviour according to the precepts they upheld meant auto-
matic material and spiritual rewards—one only has to look at

the biblical book of Proverbs to find this straightforward and uncomplicated view of life. Proverbs 10:17 provides an example—'He who heeds instruction is on the path to life, but he who rejects reproof goes astray'. There is a certain security in such certainty. And yet it is often the case that if faith in God is based on simplistic foundations, at the first real suffering it stumbles and falls. However, it is also the case that for many people a straightforward, uncomplicated way of looking at things is more palatable and in the end works better for them.

There are many examples of suffering leading to loss of belief in God—some Jews, for example, when the Holocaust happened, couldn't believe that God could permit such unspeakable suffering. Not only did people feel that God had abandoned them, they no longer felt able to believe in him. One Jew expressed the reaction of many to the horrors of Auschwitz when he wrote: 'The executioner killed for nothing, the victim died for nothing. No God ordered the one to prepare the stake, nor the other to mount it. At Auschwitz the sacrifices were without point. If the suffering of one human being has any meaning, that of six million has none'. The traditional Jewish answer, found in the Old Testament, was that if you were suffering you must have sinned in some way. This was the obvious corollary to the theory that if you were good you would prosper. But sometimes the punishment far exceeds the crime, and many felt that the Holocaust was in this category. The Holocaust was a case of innocent suffering—the people could never have 'deserved' such a fate on such a scale, whatever they had done.

Yet there was another kind of reaction: for some the suffering in a curious way strengthened them and their faith. I am reminded of Corrie Ten Boom's true story told in her book *The*

Hiding Place, in which she writes of her and her sister's imprisonment in Ravensbruck. They smuggled a Bible in and man-
aged to keep it hidden, and it provided for them a sustenance
that they had never imagined they could feel in such a situation. She writes, 'The blacker the night around us grew, the
brighter and truer and more beautiful burned the word of God'.
For some, the suffering led them to find a faith they had not
previously had. Corrie Ten Boom talks of a growing group of
people wanting to join in their meetings, so many that they
had more than one session a day in which they were engaged in
reading the Bible and in praying together. She herself never
lost sight of God throughout the experience of suffering—she
found that God was there for her in her time of need. This
raises the question of whether God can be found in the midst
of suffering, even in the kind of suffering that just seems senseless or cruel. These words scratched onto the wall of his cell by
a Jew show that faith stayed alive even in the midst of despair: 'I
believe in the sun even when it's not shining. I believe in love
even when not feeling it. I believe in God even when he is silent…'.

Some Jews at the time of the Holocaust had the feeling that
God was hiding his face from his people, as expressed in Psalm
44:24, where the psalmist asks God 'Why dost thou hide thy
face? Why dost thou forget our affliction and oppression?' Others quite simply felt outraged and angry, and their reaction was
one of protest against God for having seemingly forgotten them,
as expressed in Psalm 22:2: 'O my God, I cry by day, but thou
dost not answer; and by night, but find no rest'. For some their
anger led them to reject God, whilst for others it was a curious
route to a deeper and more meaningful relationship with him.
R. S. Thomas, a Welsh priest and poet, expresses both these

reactions in a defiant question to God in his poem 'AD' in the book entitled *Counterpoint:* 'What makes you God but the free-dom you have given us to bellow our defiance at you over the grave's maw, or to let silence ensue so deliberately as to be taken for an Amen?' Whether your suffering leads you to reject or embrace God, there is clearly a great deal of anger and protest and conflict to be worked out along the way in the process of trying to understand.

The reaction which I want particularly to explore in this book is the last one I have mentioned, the anger and protest that all people feel in the face of suffering—not just anger with God but anger with the world and other people. In the television play *Goodbye Cruel World,* Barbara discovers that she is dying of a wasting disease. Her husband, Roy, goes through a whole range of reactions: he refuses to accept the diagnosis, he thinks that by working to set up a charity to find a cure he can save his wife, he goes through a period of rejection of his wife and the disease she represents, he refuses to help her, he feels anger and despair and blames others along the way. Throughout the whole ordeal he feels that her suffering is unfair and undeserved, but in the end they are drawn closer together in the midst of the suffering and, when she inevitably dies, he gradually becomes calmer and more accepting. He finds a way of seeing his char-ity work in the broader context of helping others rather than just Barbara. He grows as a person through the suffering, even though he still cannot understand why this has happened to them. His experience shows that whilst anger and protest can be negative and lead to despair, it can also have a positive side. Out of anger can spring a deeper understanding and the strength and the will to change things.

Rather than raise unanswerable questions in this book and

attempt to find definitive answers, I shall look at different reactions to suffering and try to explore the reasons behind them.
By this approach I hope to provoke fresh thought and to explore new avenues of possibility. In raising and addressing many
of the issues in the context of the Old Testament book of Job I
shall try to show that it has a profound contribution to make
to our understanding of the baffling issues raised by suffering,
which are so enormous in their complexity and yet so central
and personal in our lives.

2

Why Job?

Mr Zuss: Oh, there's always
  someone playing Job.
Nickles: There must be
  Thousands! What's that got to do with it?
  Thousands—not with camels either:
  Millions and millions of mankind
  Burned, crushed, broken, mutilated,
  Slaughtered, and for what? For thinking!
  For walking round the world in the wrong
  Skin, the wrong-shaped noses, eyelids:
  Sleeping the wrong night wrong city—
  London, Dresden, Hiroshima.
  There never could have been so many
  Suffered more for less....

  A. MacLeish, *JB*

The book of Job has inspired many writers, artists and thinkers over the centuries. The opening passage comes from a 1950s existentialist play inspired by the book of Job entitled *JB*. Here at the start of the play two minor characters, Mr Zuss and Nickles, are having a preliminary discussion about the hero, JB, before the main action of the play begins. This is a common technique amongst playwrights— Shakespeare's plays, for example, invariably begin with a conversation between minor characters which leads the audience gradually, almost imperceptibly, into the main plot of the play. Here, Mr Zuss and Nickles are setting the stage and creating the conditions in which the play will evolve. They give the audience a taste of the action that is going to follow, rather like the prologue to a Greek play. They are making it clear here that it is no extraordinary occurrence that a person should suffer— it happens every day to innocent people and for no good reason. This enables MacLeish to make the point that JB is in a sense Everyman because he is representative of others in situations of suffering. It is also a means of telling the audience that JB is going to suffer before the play has even started, before JB himself knows it—the situation is all planned out in advance and the audience are let into the secret. This effect is known as dramatic irony—the audience know the fate of the victim before he does, and everything subsequent is able to be interpreted with this 'secret' knowledge in mind. This gives the effect of watching a play within a play which leads the audience to suspend disbelief in what is going to follow. Presumably MacLeish took the idea for this technique from the real book of Job.

The book of Job is often regarded as the most profound book on suffering in the Bible. It has been described as the 'Matterhorn' of the Old Testament in the way it addresses a very difficult set of questions in a manner that is not simplistic. Why choose the book of Job to study today? I choose Job not because he is a particular case history but because, like JB in the play, he is Everyman. I shall try to show the way in which the strange dual character presented in the book, and the questions and answers raised by its author, make it a broader and more profound study than a mere case history would be. In the book is contained not just one but a number of responses to suffering. As in life, many profound questions are raised and yet no easy answers are given.

Clearly the book of Job was written a long time ago and is conditioned to a certain extent by its context in time. No longer in the West do we measure wealth in number of camels and cattle. Yet, human nature and human experience do not basically change and hence the book can be relevant to us today. Job is traditionally seen as part of the 'wisdom literature' of the Old Testament, literature which also includes Proverbs, and which sprang from a universal quest to understand human nature, God and the world. Rather than accept the simple answers of the wisdom tradition about how to understand life as Proverbs maintains, however, the author of Job challenged the very presuppositions of that tradition. The author realized that situations of suffering raise fundamental questions about the meaning of human life and our relationship with God. So, the book challenged accepted beliefs of its day in a profound way—and it can likewise challenge us today.

On the face of it the book of Job tells a simple tale of a man who 'feared God and turned away from evil' (Job 1:1). He was a good and kind man who went out of his way to help others, who kept up religious observances, who tried to lead a decent and upright life as far as possible. He sounds like many ordinary people living today. Although our society is not as religious as his was, there is still a strong will amongst people to lead a good life. Even if we are not particularly religious and don't go to church on Sundays, most of us have a sense of trying to hold on to some kind of integrity of our own and trying to treat other people well and to spread a little happiness if we can.

The issue is that despite this attempt to lead a good life, calamity strikes. It can happen to anybody at any time, with no explanation and for no reason. It can happen suddenly in a car crash or a bankruptcy, or more slowly in a marriage breakdown or a painful death from cancer. In Job's case the calamities happened suddenly and in rapid succession. First his children died as the result of a natural disaster, and then he lost all his possessions, his cattle and his livelihood. Then he lost his dignity by being struck down by a wasting disease. Despite having tried to lead a good life, he lost status, possessions, self-respect and, perhaps most tragic of all, he lost his children. It is that old feeling of unfairness I spoke of in the first chapter. Somehow for Job the balance seems to have tilted in the direction of calamity way above the odds. It is clear that Job certainly did not deserve what came to him. How was he then to come to terms with what had happened?

The story of Job in the prologue to the book also takes us

behind the earthly scene to the heavenly court. Here we, the audience, are suddenly let in on part of the story of which Job is unaware. We are in the realm of the dramatic irony I was talking about in relation to JB. Just as MacLeish used Mr Zuss and Nickles to tell us of the suffering that would befall JB, so the author of the prologue tells us of a wager that took place in heaven between God and Satan, which seems to explain why Job is suffering. He is the victim of a bet between God and Satan over whether he would or would not waver from his faith if faced with calamity. This is clearly a scenario about which Job knows nothing. As with JB we, the audience, are here being given an insight into 'behind-the-scenes' action. Rather as MacLeish is asking a play within a play to be performed, the author of Job is providing us with an introduction that conditions the way we read the rest of the book. The story may have already existed in the folk memory of the people with this wager as one of its ingredients, or maybe it is a literary device— the author of Job perhaps decided that such a heavenly prologue was necessary to provide the audience or reader with an explanation for Job's suffering. If either the folk tradition or the author had not included in the story this reason for Job's suffering then there would have been a more chilling prospect to face, that perhaps the answer to why Job suffered these calamities is that there is no reason… We shall see how the author does not rest at this solution alone, which suggests that he thought that the issues were more profound than this simple tale of a wager allowed for.

God says to Satan in the prologue, 'Have you considered my servant Job, that there is none like him on the earth, a blameless and upright man, who fears God and turns away from evil?' Clearly God knows that Job is a steadfast, faithful man but Satan suggests that Job is only faithful to God because of his prosperity. Satan replies with a question, followed by a statement and then by a challenge: 'Does Job fear God for naught? Hast thou not put a hedge about him and his house and all that he has, on every side? Thou hast blessed the work of his hands, and his possessions have increased in the land. But put forth thy hand now, and touch all that he has, and he will curse thee to thy face'. It becomes quickly apparent that this wager is designed to test Job's faith.

An accusation sometimes levelled at religious people is that they are only in it for what they can get out of it. It is as if religion provides some kind of insurance policy against calamity—believe in God and all will work out fine. This is the argument Satan uses in the prologue—the only reason Job has tried to lead a good life, Satan claims, is because he thought God would protect him against calamity. What otherwise is the point of leading a good life at all? He has to have some motive and this must be it. It couldn't be, argues Satan, that Job is doing so for no reason, that his righteousness is disinterested. The presupposition is that people always have a selfish motive for doing things—those who help others are often criticized in this way. The woman who visits the old lady every week, for example, is sometimes unfairly accused of being motivated purely by an interest in her money when she dies. God, on the other hand, remains convinced that Job indeed is acting disinterestedly.

Satan's first question is this: Would Job not waver from his faith in God if all his possessions and loved ones were taken away from him? The answer to the question is to inflict this suffering on Job and see what happens. Satan does this but it quickly becomes apparent that this test is not enough. Job is still maintaining a pious stance that infuriates Satan. Job holds on to faith despite this calamity. After the first round of testing is successful God says to Satan, 'He still holds fast his integrity, although you moved me against him, to destroy him without cause'. God is convinced of Job's disinterested righteousness; however, it appears that Satan is not. Satan asks a further question: Would Job not waver if he was struck down by a festering disease? This is stage two. Job is afflicted with a leprous disease in which pus-filled blisters keep appearing, growing and then bursting to spread further infection and to fill with maggots and worms. Whilst no one is sure exactly what Job's disease was (and it is likely today that we would be able to cure it), that observation does not lessen the impact of the kind of physical suffering he must have endured. Furthermore, whilst we have painkillers in today's world, which would no doubt have eased the situation considerably for Job, this does not obscure the point that some people live with real, unceasing pain all the time. There is never any respite from it, it nags and nags until it frays the nerves and the temper and starts to dominate the thoughts and mind of the one suffering the pain. Job's illness sounds similar to the plague that swept through England in the seventeenth century—the plague too caused pus-filled blisters to cover the body. The disease spread like wildfire, and all houses containing a plague victim were obliged to mark their door with a red cross. This meant that the house became isolated, ignored, and the people within it became outcasts and unclean. At Eyam there was an outbreak of the plague in 1665, and the entire village made themselves outcasts in order to prevent it from spreading to other parts of Derbyshire. There is a tale of immense self-sacrifice to be told here—two hundred and sixty villagers died, and only fifteen survived the ordeal.

It is sometimes said by disabled or handicapped people today that they feel in a sense rejected by others in society—talked down to or ignored as if they were less than human. This is also true for people suffering from a contagious disease. As recently as forty years ago small children with such diseases were kept in isolation hospitals, away from even their parents. This potentially had quite damaging psychological side effects. Thus physical illness can lead to mental illness and feelings of rejection. So Job too not only develops a terrible disease but he is abhorrent to his wife and an outcast from the city. He is to be found sitting on a dungheap outside the city scratching his sores—a sad plunge into poverty, disease and calamity for a man who was respected by all and was an upright citizen. Job has become a pathetic, pitiful figure. Yet his one strength is that despite all this misfortune and suffering, both mental and physical, he retains his faith in God. He is prepared to accept misfortune from God as he accepted prosperity—he is a model of patience which is almost unreal. We might ask how many people today would react to such suffering in this patient way.

Job also seems to be the victim of a bet, which makes his plight even more unfair. God allowed Satan to test Job's patience to find out his real motives for leading a good life. We might ask not only how a loving God could ever subject his followers to such a test—I am reminded of the story of Abraham and Isaac in which Abraham goes through the torment of being about to sacrifice his son at God's behest and, only as he is poised to kill him, does God grant a reprieve. This story raises the question, What kind of God subjects his faithful believers to such trials? In the prologue of Job, why does God allow Satan such power? It is as if God is allowing evil free rein. Is that in fact what God does? Is this story actually expressing the truth that God cannot prevent evil from happening to people? Does it show that his power is limited? Or does Satan represent the other side of the coin—is God simply allowing humanity to exercise free will? It is clear that fundamental problems are raised by the story which relate to our own questions about why undeserved suffering occurs.

'Does Job fear God for naught?' asks Satan, and it is the purpose of the test to find this out. Job seemingly passes the test with flying colours. When his wife advises him to 'Curse God and die' he does no such thing. He says humbly, 'Shall we receive good at the hand of God, and shall we not receive evil?' (2:10). He accepts all that comes to him, good and bad alike. Then three friends come to comfort him and sit with him silently. The end of the story is contained in the epilogue to the book. It is rather like the 'happy ending' we come to expect from fairy tales. The conditions that held before the test are restored, and not only restored but doubled. So Job is rewarded by God with a new set of children and twice as many material possessions as he had before.

There is a slight feeling of dissatisfaction with this ending—it seems to be deliberately unrealistic and heavily ironic. A new set of children sounds all very well but would we ever feel the same about them as the original ones? Furthermore, having just gone through such an ordeal of suffering how satisfied would we be with such comforts suddenly restored as if nothing had happened? Whilst a positive side of suffering can be that people grow through it, there is often a feeling that one can never go back to what was before. We have started on a journey which is one-way and whilst we might hanker for what went before, recognition that things will never be quite the same again is the first step in the healing and acceptance process.

Well, we can make concessions and say that this is only a

story. And it would be a straightforward enough folk-tale-type story if that were all, but in fact we have only seen what is contained in the prose prologue and epilogue to the book of Job. There are thirty-nine chapters of dialogue in between. In the dialogue section we suddenly meet a character who starkly contrasts with the rather bland, accepting figure we have just met. We find a man cursing and protesting and bewailing his innocence. We find three friends who suddenly stop being silent and are full of stock answers. We find Elihu, a young intruder into the debate who seems to come from nowhere and disappear after four chapters without further mention (a section often regarded as a later addition to the book by another author and so not discussed here), and we find speeches from none other than God himself which speak of his power in creation and do not appear to have much to do with the questions being asked by Job. We find a book that is most probably based on a real experience of suffering or at least on a profound knowledge of what suffering involves. We therefore find a book that should not perhaps be laid aside quite as easily as we have almost been tempted to do.

So, in the dialogue the figure of patience is gone and a new rebellious Job has found his way into our narrative. This raises the question, Who was Job? Did he have a split personality or do we in fact have two different people here? How can we reconcile the patient, accepting man of the prologue with the protesting figure of the dialogue? Did he suddenly change his mind or is it more complex than that? I suggest we look for an answer to this in the way the book might have come together. Just as MacLeish constructed a play within a play, we have noticed that, in being let into the secret of the wager in the prologue of Job, this author did a similar thing. We can then go a stage further and see the whole prologue section as forming the 'outer play' within which the 'inner play' (the dialogue) takes place. It seems that the author of the dialogue section may well have used an older story which he decided to retain, placing it around his own inner story to form an introduction and conclusion which actually gave a different perspective from the one he wanted to give. The whole reason for writing a dialogue at all was that the author did not feel that the outer story gave the full picture—it did not bring to life the real character and the real emotions of a man enduring great suffering.

One might want to ask the question at this point—Was Job a historical figure? All this talk of authors—is the Bible not regarded as a record of events that actually happened? Well, much of the Bible has a high claim to be historical, but in the wisdom literature, of which Job is generally held to be a part, it is likely that we are in the realm of story, told for the purpose of teaching or example. We can probably hold that the story of a patient sufferer called Job is an old one, maybe even originating from as long ago as 2000 BC and transmitted orally through tribes and peoples, down to the time of the author of the dialogue who probably lived sometime after 400 BC. It may be that there is a historical figure being spoken of here, but we have no proof of that. More significant is the story itself and what its message is. The author of the dialogue clearly felt that the older story did not say all there was to say about suffering and the kind of protest that springs out of it, and so he added his own inner story in dialogue form to the older tale and incorporated the two together.

The one fact we know about Job from outside the book of Job is from the book of Ezekiel. We know from Ezekiel that a pious character called Job, who was known for his righteousness, existed, either in actuality or in folklore, before ever the book that bears his name did. Ezekiel 14:14ff lists Job with Noah and Daniel as a righteous man—'even if these three men, Noah, Daniel, and Job, were in it [the land], they would deliver but their own lives by their righteousness, says the Lord God'. The book of Ezekiel was probably written in the sixth century BC, before the book of Job in its final form appeared. This would then support the theory that the author used an older story as the framework for his own—it would reflect the tradition of an early prose tale about a pious character called Job and leave the rebellious figure as the creation of our author.

The older story basically told of a righteous man who remained steadfast in the face of suffering. Then I suggest that around the fourth century BC an author saw the potential of this simple, well-known tale for saying something more profound about suffering, about protest and about the relationship between God and humanity. After giving his readers or listeners this starting point with which they would have been familiar, he then challenged them by filling the middle of the story with a dialogue section, which suddenly brings the character of Job to life in a startling way. This later author clearly thought that the older story was not profound enough in its treatment of the problem of Job's suffering and that the wager between God and Satan was not a satisfactory answer to why Job suffered, nor was such patience in the face of suffering. He saw that this was not the reaction of most people—perhaps that observation arose from having suffered and known the anguish, the anger and the feeling of downright unfairness that suffering engendered. Furthermore, this author wanted to write a 'real' story about suffering and create a main character to whom people could relate.

So this author creates a very different impatient Job who comes bursting in unannounced in chapter 3 of the book, doing just what his wife told him to do—cursing! As Stephen Mitchell vividly translates the opening words of chapter 3: 'Finally Job cried out, "God damn the day I was born"'—desperate words coming from the depths of a person's despair. Suddenly the character of Job comes alive. No longer do we have a pious, bland character who simply accepts good and bad, here we have someone protesting at none other than God himself. Any thought of Satan is gone—it is God who in Job's eyes has inflicted this undeserved suffering and he is to be held to account.

A major frustration for those who suffer and for those who care for them is the feeling of not understanding what has happened. There is a need gradually to come to an understanding but at first this seems impossible. It is often small, unexpected events or words that suddenly come to mean something, maybe long after they have occurred or been spoken, and that seem to lead to some solace or some kind of answer. Job too basically does not understand why he is suffering. He feels he ought to be able to understand, and in fact the dialogue section is mainly concerned with wrestling with himself to understand his situation. However it is a 'dialogue' and the dialogue is with others, namely three so-called friends or comforters who try to comfort him by providing explanations. But Job finds that their explanations do not address the new issues raised for him by his suffering. How often do we find this—that friends who only mean to be kind often do not see the real issues or address the heart of our anguish? People try to help but the upset to life is such that recovery really needs to come gradually and largely from within. Job's world has been turned upside-down—no

longer are the pat answers the friends give sufficient. Job has
moved on from their position and come to see his life and his
relationship to God in a different way.

The stance taken by the friends is that all the calamities which
are happening to Job constitute his punishment for having
sinned. People who suffered God's punishment must have
sinned—that was the accepted answer to suffering. It is an answer that is often given today—people feel that calamity has
come to right some wrong done in the past, and there is a feeling that the suffering is in a sense deserved. But Job maintains
that he is innocent—he does not deserve this suffering. Of that
he is sure, as he sits on his dunghill scratching his sores and as
he contemplates all that he has lost.

Interestingly, the speeches of the friends gradually get shorter
and those of Job get longer as he gains ground and leaves their
arguments behind. The dialogue almost imperceptibly changes
from a confrontation between Job and the friends to a confrontation between Job and God. After all, Job sees God as the
real source of his anguish. Why should a just and fair-minded
God have inflicted this suffering on one as faithful as Job? Eventually Job's only plea is for God to appear to him. He has the
feeling that if only somehow he can be made to understand
why these things have happened to him he will be able to bear
the suffering. He wants God to justify his ways—what right, he
asks, has God to be so inconsistent? At last towards the end of
the book God appears but the sting in the tail—rather like a
story by Roald Dahl—is that he quite simply ignores Job's questions. He asks Job where he was at creation and why he thinks
he has a right to all the answers. So God was there for Job in the
end, but he was not there in the way that Job expected.

Does Job get any kind of real answer? It is true that—like a good detective story—the answer can sometimes be the one we are not looking for and least expect. This answer does not seem to be on a rational or intellectual level anyway—and maybe Job was wrong to seek it there. Perhaps Job gained new strength as a result of his trials. Or has he reached a more profound understanding of God? Perhaps he has, since he feels moved to repent and states that he has uttered what he did not understand. In the presence of God he is humbled and then God tells the friends that Job has spoken 'what is right' (42:7) in contrast to them—an odd statement by God at this point which appears to vindicate Job as we have seen, in renewed prosperity: the restoration of Job's fortunes with double what he had before. It is in fact the end of not just one story but of two, the first of a patient uncomplaining Job and the second of an impatient Job. Unlike the novel by John Fowles, *The French Lieutenant's Woman,* which has two alternative endings, a happy and a sad one, the book of Job has one ending but is made up of two stories.

3

Job the Patient Sufferer

You have heard of the steadfastness of Job, and
you have seen the purpose of the Lord, how the
Lord is compassionate and merciful.

James 5:11

It is rare in life that we actually meet someone who suffers without complaint and with an air of calmness and acceptance which is genuine. Such a response seems almost unreal and yet it does happen occasionally. Dietrich Bonhoeffer was one such person. With a profound sense of faith in a suffering God, he wrote whilst in prison for his beliefs, 'I must admit candidly I sometimes feel almost ashamed of how much we talk about our own suffering'. This kind of calm, prayerful reaction can generate in us a feeling of anger. I have always felt sympathetic towards Job's wife, who when Job is at his most pious, tells him to 'Curse God'—she is the angry one both on her own account and on his.

For centuries, beginning with the New Testament epistle of James, the inner story contained in the book—the 'rebellious' Job—was largely ignored. All we find is such references to Job as the model of patience. The epistle of James was probably written only about five centuries after the main dialogue section of the book of Job. So, it is especially interesting that as early as this, Job is held up as an example of how to behave in the face of suffering. His rebelliousness is felt to be less appropriate for those turning to the book for guidance. The outer story demonstrates that to suffer patiently, as Job did, is the appropriate response, for God is merciful and will have compassion. Life may have its trials and tribulations but, like Job, when you have passed the test, you will be rewarded by God. It is this kind of simplistic reading of the book that seems to me to have given Job a bad press today. Even now, people read the book as if that was its real message.

It seems then that from very early times some people found the rebelliousness hard to swallow. A strain of protest, that enabled the author to bring the character of Job to life in the inner story, became irrelevant to the pious of a later period. So traditions built up that hid the 'true' story behind layers of legend and embellishment. And they persist today—ask anyone who Job was and, unless they get him muddled with Jonah and start referring to the great fish, they will generally quote the phrase from the epistle of James, 'the patience of Job'. Ironically enough, this phrase has worked its way into our language to denote someone who is extremely patient. In this book I hope to undo that misconception.

It is interesting that even in the modern drama and music inspired by Job, it is the Job of the outer story who still persists. Ralph Vaughan Williams composed *Job (a masque for dancing)* inspired by the book of Job, and yet the moods of the music and its themes are entirely based on the outer prose story. Georges de la Tour painted a beautiful picture of *Job visited by his wife,* again based on that scene in the prologue. In the play *JB* mentioned in the last chapter, it is the 'patient Job' who is to be found, whilst his wife is the one who is impatient. JB is the one who remains steadfast whilst all around him collapses. He has moments of anguish, of asking why but he never wavers from the basic position of trust in God and faithfulness to him. His wife is given the character that is hinted at in the outer story of the biblical book of Job—she is prepared to give up on God in the face of the calamity, a natural enough reaction perhaps on the part of one watching a loved one suffer. But JB is the model of patience. JB says to his wife (Sarah in the play): 'Shall we take the good and not the evil? We have to take the chances, Sarah: evil with good. It doesn't mean there is no good!' MacLeish introduces a new element here to the argument— the question of chance, an issue that is implied but not explicitly raised in the biblical book of Job.

In the last chapter we asked why the author of the dialogue thought it necessary to add any more to the older story, and suggested that it was because he saw the potential in making a simple tale more profound. The simple tale is about patience in the face of suffering and one might well argue that in fact that is a very valid response. What better than to remain calm in the face of suffering and accept it? Acceptance is surely sensible because in fact by the time the suffering has been inflicted, by the time the car accident, for example, has happened, it is too late to do anything about it. We have seen, however, how the accepting Job is rather a bland character, in contrast to the protesting Job of the dialogue. Does this suggest that acceptance and patience is a less valid response?

I think the answer is that it is not by any means a less valid response—in fact it is a worthy response if one can really behave in this way. Whilst there may be people who can bear misfortune stoically and without great complaint, I think the reason why this kind of characterization may seem bland is that most people are not like that. When calamity strikes there are very few who can show an attitude of acceptance right from the start. It may be that acceptance is the final stage of response after much pain and grief and lament along the way but there is rarely this kind of reaction from the start. MacLeish realized that in his play. Whilst he wanted to portray the patient Job, he does so by combining with the characterization elements of doubt and grief and anguish which make Job into a real person. In the same way the author of the dialogue must have asked the question, How many people are really like that? Some people may be accepting types who take knocks and blows without complaint, but they are few and far between. In this chapter then we will explore aspects of this accepting reaction to suffering, not intending to devalue it, since it is laudable if it can be sustained, but realizing that, like the character of the patient Job, it is almost an impossible reaction for many people in real situations of suffering.

I mentioned earlier that some people can hold on to faith whilst suffering, and the experience in some curious way strengthens them. First of all, faith in God enables the process of acceptance of the suffering and then, once some kind of acceptance has occurred, the path is clear for an exploration of a deeper kind of faith, as Corrie Ten Boom discovered. The process of acceptance often results in a new energy to try to bring good out of the suffering. We hear many examples of outstanding human courage and forbearance in our modern world which suggest that the human spirit is not to be crushed. For many people suffering leads eventually to a new strength and will to go on. That is not to say that suffering is good or necessary. It is just that good can come out of it.

There is a line of thought that feels suffering to be a 'higher path' which may be related to the easier acceptance of suffering that we see in some people. Mr Zuss in MacLeish's play *JB* says, 'Isn't there anything you understand? It's from the ash heap God is seen. Always! Always from the ashes. Every saint and martyr knew that!' The inference is that one cannot truly know God unless one has suffered, and so suffering is to be embraced as a way to God. The mention of saints and martyrs is apt here—we could find many examples of saints and martyrs who seemed to bear suffering, mental and physical, with remarkable calm. Of course they also had great faith in the life to come after death, a doctrine that is less readily accepted today. But even so, they showed immense endurance in the face of lions, and other less feline persecutors. Many Christians over the centuries have adopted this view that to suffer as God suffered in Christ is in a sense to draw nearer to God and to faith in him.

Whilst it is incredible what people can endure when they are tortured both mentally and physically—one only has to think of the limits reached by those held hostage or the great feats undertaken by explorers—few today would opt for such a path or think that it put them on a higher plane than other people. There are still some people who have a saintly quality about them, who seem to be able to bear 'the slings and arrows of outrageous fortune' without complaint, but that is probably not true of the majority of us. It may be that our levels of endurance are higher than we think they are—sometimes when you think you have reached the limits of what you can endure another calamity occurs to push those limits even further. But most people have their breaking point. However, not, it seems, the Job of the prologue. When the first set of calamities is not enough to break him, the second set arrives and his limits of endurance are stretched even further, and yet even that does not break him. There is a quality to the character of Job here that is saintly—patient but also pious, almost annoyingly pious. The irritation we might feel when reading this story is a common reaction to very calm, poised, accepting sufferers. We want to ask of the patient Job, 'Does the man have no word of complaint to make?' It reminds me again of Abraham standing poised to sacrifice his son, Isaac, and uttering no word as he lifts the knife. What kind of forbearance was that? One sometimes comes across a person who is really saintly and seems to have a deep trust in God. Perhaps we want to ask, 'How can you be so sure? Where does this certainty come from? Why don't I feel it?'

However, there are those who hold to the view that suffering has a purificatory quality, that you cannot really know yourself, or others, or God, if you have not suffered. This line of argument could have all kinds of repercussions for medical matters—if pain is somehow a good thing, should we be treating it? We can think in this context of physical pain—cancer, for example—but we can also think of mental pain such as the mental scars left by war or imprisonment. There are those who are against treating pain and even against performing operations, but they are in a minority. I suggest that many people today would question the value of this kind of argument in view of the progress we have made in treating pain. It is true that often people who appear to be in great physical pain seem to have a greater scope for endurance, but again I don't think that anyone would willingly opt for such a path.

To take this argument in a different direction: it can be seen to be related to the reaction I mentioned in my first chapter, that when life is going too well there is the feeling that one deserves a little misfortune. It is true, as we shall go on to explore, that one often grows as a person through suffering, but again that should not make us want to embrace it with open arms. Suffering may bring one into tune with new, unknown depths in one's personality that can sometimes be very frightening. Prisoners and hostages such as Terry Waite, Brian Keenan and John McCarthy have found, for example, that the sudden experience of solitude for the first time in their lives can bring them to the edge of insanity, but it can also mean that, for the first time, they know their own limits and have to cope with themselves. Self-knowledge of this kind can be desirable or not—it may well be that through suffering one might come to know oneself better in a positive way. However, I don't think many of us would actively wish to find out about ourselves by this means or see it as some kind of explanation of why suffering has been inflicted upon us.

Suffering has sometimes been seen as a test of faith, and this is still true today. God is seen to be testing people of faith in the same way that he tested Job. In the prose story, the patient Job is tested on the issue of disinterested righteousness. His motivation for trusting God is questioned. We might pause to look at our motives for trusting God. Do we do so because in some strange way we think things might turn out better for us? Are we looking forward to receiving a passport to heaven? Do we think that it will mean life is more prosperous for us? Or are our motives more disinterested? Do we genuinely trust God because he is God and because we believe in the revelation he has given to us? Do we accept him expecting nothing and taking the rough with the smooth? Are we prepared then to suffer and to look to God for strength in that suffering rather than blaming him?

The hardest path to travel along is the path towards acceptance and yet that is the one we need eventually to take if we are not to be hardened or embittered or crushed. This is the route I shall explore in the remaining chapters of this book. Rather than accepting suffering in an unreasoned, passive kind of way, most of us have to travel a more tortuous path. It is not a better path, it is just a process of stages, rather like the stages of grief people go through after a bereavement. We may end up at the same point as the patient Job, as the saints and martyrs or as those whom we rather envy at their calm in the face of calamity. But we may not. In the next chapter I shall look at the first stage of the journey—the attempt to rationalize the situation.

4

Rationalizing
the Situation—
Job and the Friends

Teach me, and I will be silent;
Make me understand how I have erred.
Job 6:24

Whenever anything happens to us we try to rationalize it. Perhaps the reason suffering is such a difficult problem is that we try to rationalize something that cannot be rationalized. We try to solve something intellectually that is not of that nature. Yet with our powers of reasoning that is hardly surprising. It is a curious paradox that we have been given these powers of reasoning and yet all too often find ourselves tip against the limits of that reason. The process of rationalizing is an important stage in the acceptance process. It is a natural human reaction to need to find reasons why something has happened. It is also natural to want to find a scapegoat or someone to blame, even if we come to realize that this is not the final answer.

When we face difficult times and seek to understand our reactions, each of us has to start from who we are, where we are from, what has made us the way we are and who or what has influenced us in life. All of us have certain beliefs or fixed points in our lives, and we need to hold on to those even harder when we suffer, even if, in the end, it becomes apparent that holding on is making our situation worse and that in fact we no longer believe what we used to uphold so fervently. We have therefore to rationalize our situation within a framework of existing belief and holding on to certain presuppositions. We need a starting point for our deliberations.

Job's framework of existing belief is represented by the wise men whose views are to be found in the wisdom literature of the Old Testament, the book of Proverbs in particular. This literature was the product of human experience within the Israelite religious tradition—human reasoning if you like. Those who were wise in Israel observed the world and found patterns and orders in it. They advocated the idea of the two paths—one to life, goodness, prosperity, wisdom, and the other to death, evil, poverty and failure. Each person could choose which path to walk along—good deeds leading to life, bad ones to death. The book of Job, however, counters this idea by stating that the world does not conform to such an easy pattern. The experience of the author of Job teaches him the opposite of what the wise who went before him had maintained. In the book therefore all Job's presuppositions are overturned by his experience of suffering. That the just and the wicked get their correct rewards, says Job, is just not true. He states that God destroys both the blameless and the wicked. His evidence for this accusation is that he himself is blameless and yet he is being wrongly punished. Job says in 9:21–24: 'I am blameless; I regard not myself; I loathe my life. It is all one; therefore I say, he destroys both the blameless and the wicked. When disaster brings sudden death, he mocks at the calamity of the innocent. The earth is given into the hand of the wicked; he covers the faces of its judges—if it is not he, who then is it?' So his conclusion is that God must treat wicked and blameless alike. Moreover, it even seems that the wicked are not punished since they appear to do nothing but prosper—'How often is it that the lamp of the wicked is put out?' Job asks. 'That their calamity comes upon them? That God distributes pains in his anger?' (21:17).

There is a problem here that we are all familiar with—it is

all very well thinking that good things come to those who are pious, but doesn't experience often contradict this presupposition? Doesn't experience often teach us that prosperity very often comes to those who are not pious at all but rather to those, for example, who mistreat or persecute others or use criminal means to secure their money? The author of Psalm 73 was aware of this problem—'Behold, these are the wicked; always at ease, they increase in riches. All in vain have I kept my heart clean and washed my hands in innocence' (v.12)—also aware of it is the author of Job in the dialogue. Does this strange reversal of justice mean that God is unjust? That must be the answer—and yet it is inconceivable….This is the way Job's reasoning goes. In the process of trying to rationalize his situation he ends up with a different set of questions for which he is striving to find answers.

Despite our inkling that maybe there is no strict pattern of justice at work concerning rewards and punishments, as Job perceived, the belief that 'good' is somehow on our side and that our actions affect the way things turn out is a strong one.

Otherwise, it is argued, why lead a moral life at all? For many people, good actions are at the heart of their faith, others just try to lead a good life for no real reason apart from the fact that they hope people will do the same to them. There is not necessarily the idea of reward as the main aim of such a stance, but there is often a feeling of 'bad things won't happen to me' which shakes the faith of some when misfortune strikes or leads to a cynicism that whatever one does doesn't make any difference. In the play *JB* there is a running debate between JB and his wife about getting what you deserve. At the start of the play, when they are prospering, Sarah, JB's wife, holds that their prosperity is a matter of desert:

Sarah: If anyone deserved it you do.
JB: That's not true. I don't deserve it.
      It's not a question of deserving.
Sarah: Oh it is. That's all the question.
      However could we sleep at night…
JB: Nobody *deserves* it, Sarah:
      Not the world that God has given us.
(There is a moment's strained silence, then JB is laughing)
      But I believe in it, Sal. I trust in it.
      I trust my luck—my life—our life—
      God's goodness to me.

Sarah's response is to say that JB can only trust his luck because he has deserved it. JB still maintains that we receive gifts from God, good and bad alike, free of charge. Later, when they have lost all four children, JB holds on to faith and portrays a picture of God suffering alongside them:

      Sarah!
Even desperate we can't despair—
Let go each other's fingers—sink
Numb in that dumb silence—drown there
Sole in our cold selves…
      We cannot!…
God is there too, in the desperation.
I do not know why God should strike
But God is what is stricken also:
Life is what despairs in death
and, desperate, is life still…

Sarah's response this time is to accuse God of senseless killing. She has lost her faith in the doctrine of just retribution and has lost her faith in God too. JB, in not having held to it in the same way, can find room for growth in his faith even amidst the senselessness of it all. For JB, God is suffering alongside them, God is not to be blamed....

One answer to the fact that in this life the system of just reward doesn't seem to be working is to talk about heaven. A religious motivation for centuries has been that if you do this or that good deed you will be rewarded, if not in this life, then in heaven. Nowadays, as with the doctrine of the afterlife, many people are sceptical of the concept of heaven. The picture in Job of a heavenly court where decisions are made and where God rules over the angels is one that many of us cannot relate to or accept. The idea of heaven 'out there' has been challenged by Don Cupitt, amongst others, who argues for the concept of heaven within and around us. We can help to create heaven on earth in our own lives and in the lives of others if we choose to do so—and at the end of it all there may be some kind of spiritual existence, but it will not mean going to a place out there, rather remaining here but in a different dimension. Instead of saving all our hope of heaven for a future time and despising this earthly life as many of the Fathers of the Church did, we should be seeking to make something more ideal out of our lives on earth. We can see that it is unsatisfactory for us today to talk in terms of a fair system that will be in operation when we get to heaven. It is a matter of living with the reality of the here and now, whatever the future holds.

The dialogue section of Job addresses that reality. Much of the book is concerned with opposing the easy optimism that says the good are always rewarded and the wicked suffer. Or to put it another way, that if you are prospering you must be a good person, and if you are suffering you must have sinned. The presupposition of both Job and the friends before calamity struck him was that God protects, shields and rewards those who do not sin against him. This belief was shattered for Job by the misfortunes which he and his family suffered. His friends upheld the traditional belief and could only assume that Job was guilty of a sin to which he refused to face up and confess. Job's stance was that he was innocent of the charge of sin and he became convinced that the traditional arguments put forward by the friends were based on falsehood. He was persistent in the way he threw doubt on traditional arguments in order to try to wrest from God a better answer to the great sufferings which he experienced. We shall see how in his protest he tried to move beyond these answers to new ones of his own.

The whole dialogue with the friends is on the issue of suffering as a punishment for sin. This had been an answer to the suffering endured by the Israelites at the time of the Exile. In the sixth century BC the nation was captured by an alien power, and the upper classes of society were deported to Babylon. How were the Israelites to understand this? They looked at themselves and their recent history and perceived that they were to blame. The suffering was a punishment from God for their sins. It was their responsibility and they could only blame themselves. It may well be that part of the reason our author wrote the inner story of Job was to counter this stance which says that sin is always the reason for suffering. It sometimes may be the reason, but perhaps there is no reward and punishment system which is as simple as that. Maybe it is the wrong approach to try to make people feel guilty all the time. It reminds me of some of those evangelical posters you see outside churches, telling you of your 'sinful' and 'fallen' nature and your need for 'help' or 'salvation'. They play on a person's conscience or feeling of guilt. Job maintains that he is innocent, and whilst that does not mean that he never did anything wrong, it does mean that by and large he had tried to lead a good life. The friends hold on to traditional doctrines: despite Job's perception that he had led a good life, he must have sinned otherwise the doctrine is wrong and that can't be so. They hold to a theory that provides them with straightforward answers. Some people think they have all the answers worked out—a common failing of many religious people who tend to oversimplify and be over-confident. The evangelical posters are often of this nature. This approach can prove a shaky foundation for faith when calamity strikes—it is all very well for the friends to have had all the answers to Job's suffering, but what if the calamities had happened to them?

One aspect of oversimplification is to use fixed categories into which people can be slotted. We might ask whether we can relate to these hard and fast categories of 'blameless' and 'sinful' or 'good' and 'wicked' that we find in Job. No one is ever completely good, honest, upright, kind and all those things all at once and all of the time, nor is anyone completely wicked. We are each of us more of a mixture, and there is a sense in which only caricatures of people are of one type. In fact Job is not saying that he is all good. He is prepared to accept that he might have unwittingly done something wrong, but the point is that he would like to know what it is because he was certainly not aware of it. By blameless is really meant, I think, that one is trying hard to hold on to certain principles of behaviour.

One can say generally, then, that most people are not out to harm others, commit immoral actions and so on, and in that sense they are trying to lead a good life. Often the attempt to lead a good life can reveal a profound selfishness that does not allow one to get involved in other people's misfortune, and involves too much self-analysis. It is sometimes said of people

who get too bound up in their own problems 'They are making
life hell for those around them'. Without knowing it, the failure
to look outside ourselves and to the happiness of others can
make the lives of other people miserable. Job could well be accused of being inward-looking and introspective. Perhaps we
owe it to ourselves and others to deal with adversity by looking
outside ourselves rather than becoming more and more inward-
looking, a process which, although difficult at first, often leads
to long-term self-fufilment and happiness.

I talked earlier of the need to blame someone when something bad happens. When we make a mistake, we often blame
the object or another person—all very irrational, but it makes
us feel better! Job blames God for the calamities, and rightly so
within his framework of belief. In a less religious age we are
less ready to blame God for what happens, but we still need to
blame somebody. I detect in the modern world a mood of resignation, perhaps it is an unspoken knowledge that in fact we
are to blame for a great deal of the misfortune in life. If we are
foolish enough, for example, to ride around at seventy miles
an hour in little metal boxes with engines in them, there is
bound to be the occasional accident or death, and the victims
are going to be related to someone somewhere. However, whilst
we can rationalize in that way, it is a very different thing when
the victim is your son or daughter or parent or child. Then
such rationalizing sounds like platitudes—which is just what
the speeches of the friends of Job sounded like to him. Zophar,
for example, in 11:13–14, adopts a bossy, didactic tone: 'If you
set your heart aright, you will stretch out your hands toward
him. If iniquity is in your hand, put it far away, and let not
wickedness dwell in your tents'. He is trying to be firm and tell
Job what to do—all well-meant but not what Job wanted to

hear. So, Job and the friends both start from the same point: believing that God is just, that God is powerful and that God punishes and rewards as he chooses. But whilst the friends insist that God always works according to fixed patterns that can be predicted, Job's experience, his anguish, tells him otherwise.

If misfortune strikes then we come back again to the feeling of unfairness. That feeling must itself spring from another, that generally we have tried hard, never done anything really bad and thus deserve a better lot. Perhaps if we knew we had much to be sorry about we would not feel that same sense of unfairness. Maybe that is why some people try to balance things up— 'so and so happened but I knew my luck couldn't last!' When we feel ourselves to have been treated unfairly we generally resort to legal proceedings. But how many times do we hear on the news of people feeling that the punishment given out by the judges does not meet the crime? How often have the guilty got off lightly? I think the answer is 'all too often' and, whilst our systems may be in need of reform, it is also the case that no system of justice can be fair to everyone all of the time. The same is true of God—he appears to be acting unfairly in Job's eyes and there is no court to which Job can appeal against God because God is the judge of all.

So Job feels a very strong sense of unfairness. As a result he not only blames God but he makes it clear that he expects more of God. Job wants desperately to believe in God's justice, but he will not accept punishment without knowing the cause. He starts to form a 'case' as in a legal court, but the problem is that his case is against God and God is both the accused and the judge! Job upholds that God is powerful but sees that as oppressive, allowing him to turn cruel when he wants to. He cries out, 'Know then that God has put me in the wrong, and closed his net about me' (19:6). And later he accuses God of casting him into the mire: 'I cry to thee and thou dost not answer me; I stand, and thou dost not heed me. Thou hast turned cruel to me; with the might of thy hand thou dost persecute me' (30:20–21). He decides that God indeed punishes and rewards as he chooses—the wicked are rewarded, the good are punished: 'But when I looked for good, evil came; and when I waited for light, darkness came' (30:26). The trouble is that this all seems up-side-down and does not fit in with human ideas of God's justice! Job's primary rationalization is to ask God what the cause of his suffering is, so he appeals for an answer. He asks, 'How many are my iniquities and my sins? Make me know my transgression and my sin' (13:23). Failing that, he would prefer God to use his power to crush him rather than leave him in this painful state—'that it would please God to crush me, that he would let loose his hand and cut me off!' (6:9). Alternatively, if he has indeed sinned he asks for forgiveness and appeals for mercy—'Why dost thou not pardon my transgression and take away my iniquity?' (7:21). But if that is the case he needs to know what he has done, and so he comes back full circle to the plea for an answer.

The friends are basically upholding the beliefs they have always had, as so many people do in the face of suffering. Their basic premise is that there has to be a reason for the suffering and it must be that Job has sinned, because God, in his justice, would not have punished without cause. This becomes clear in the first cycle of speeches, for example in 4:7—'Think now, who that was innocent ever perished? Or where were the up-right cut off?' So the friends regard Job as guilty. Zophar says in 11:6, 'Know then that God exacts of you less than your guilt deserves'. They even tell him that a little chastening from time to time is a good thing—'Behold, happy is the man whom God reproves; therefore despise not the chastening of the Almighty' (5:17), and in his refusal to accept what they say they see him as downright obstinate: 'How long will you say these things, and the words of your mouth be a great wind? Does God pervert justice?' (8:2–3). They maintain God's justice throughout, and think that in fact Job is more guilty and deserves more punishment than he is actually receiving. They could be seen to be a little low on sympathy. There is a hint of the sentiment 'Who are you to question? God's righteousness is greater than ours' (e.g. 22:3). It is a common answer to suffering to say that God is greater than we are and so we cannot try to understand his reasons. It is not that he doesn't have reasons—they are simply hidden from us. Job is saying rather that God punishes without any good reason at all.

Job and the friends start off by having a discussion but it gradually becomes apparent that neither side is listening to the other, nor do they want to listen. This can happen when someone is trying to be helpful and to comfort others in their grief—in the end the one grieving is almost led to shout, 'Just leave me alone!' I expect that is what Job would have preferred. Hence in modern usage the phrase 'Job's comforters' has come to mean people who mean well but are more of a hindrance than a help.

Job's speeches contain a number of criticisms of the friends which show his frustration with them. In the first cycle of speeches, Job describes Eliphaz's words as empty consolations which lack human sympathy. He hears him but finds his words tasteless, meaningless and nauseating. He rebukes the friends for reproving him and accuses them of exploiting situations to their own advantage rather than wanting to help him. He also charges them with trying to curry favour with God. God is too great to be deceived by this, he says. He will penetrate their shallow souls and see through this insincerity. He aligns the friends with the prosperous who look down on the unfortunate and excuse themselves from giving sympathy by assuming that the unfortunate have brought it upon themselves. He scorns their wisdom, saying that the beasts could have taught it to them. He scorns their beliefs and their false feeling of protection—'Your maxims are proverbs of ashes, your defences are defences of clay' (13:12).

In the second cycle of speeches the friends' criticisms of Job become correspondingly more personal. Eliphaz asserts that Job's own words condemn him—'Your own mouth condemns you, and not I; your own lips testify against you' (15:6)—and show that he has been rightly punished. He accuses Job of showing a lack of humility, since he knows no more than anyone else. He asks Job, 'Have you listened in the council of God? And do you limit wisdom to yourself?' (15:8). Bildad is offended by the lack of respect shown by Job for the friends—'Why are we counted as cattle? Why are we stupid in your sight?' (18:3). Job responds by calling them 'miserable comforters' (16:2) and uses their own words against them, though in fact his main complaint is against God.

In the third cycle Eliphaz again asserts that Job's suffering is proof of his sin because God is just. Job might think that God is indifferent but righteous people are glad he is not. If only Job would humble himself and make his peace with God, he would gain deliverance. The speeches in this cycle are muddled, and both the friends and Job start contradicting themselves. But generally we can see the same positions being upheld here, like two people having an argument with neither listening to the other. Again we find the claim that God's ways can be known but that God is greater than human beings. So how can we be so certain of being righteous in the eyes of God?

In these interchanges between Job and the friends we can see the irrational side that often enters a heated debate. We can see how personal insult helps to work out some of the frustration, and how criticizing others helps to work out the need to blame someone outside ourselves. Gradually as both sides become immune to each other's arguments, the possibility of rational interchange becomes less and the desire to criticize and become heated gets stronger. It is interesting that this aspect of human nature doesn't change!

We have begun our introduction to the rebellious Job by considering the dialogue between him and the friends. Whilst this debate on the issue of just retribution is an important theme in the book, we will go on to see that Job's protest consists of much more than this. It is clear that the friends do not come up with satisfactory answers, and that Job goes beyond the positions of the friends in the way he throws into question the religious tradition he has inherited. This suggests that we should always be prepared to ask 'why?' and to challenge accepted beliefs. Job moves his complaints to a higher judge—God—and so the dialogue starts to concern the whole nature of the God-human relationship.

Whilst many people today are persuaded to deny either God's existence or his love by what they experience or see of innocent suffering, Job's challenge and questioning was undertaken without any suggestion of not believing in God, but rather from a certainty that God was there and that he was concerned in the affairs of Job's life. Job's questioning and protest was part of his search for God and for a truer understanding of God's nature than he had previously possessed. So, it is Job the doubter that

I wish to explore at greater length—the character who does not simply accept without a word of protest what is happening to him, but who still strives for a meaningful relationship with God.

5

The Author's Protest

Parody is making new wine that tastes like the old
but has a slightly lethal effect.

D. MacDonald, Parodies

The most important aspect of any book, play or film is that we, the audience, believe in the characters. They may be eccentric, larger than life, oddities but they still need to be credible. This is where the author's skill lies—in creating a character who comes alive from the pages and makes us forget that we are involved in a story rather than reality. And yet in order to achieve this the author is in fact involved in the most subtle of literary techniques which we, if we want to understand the structures contained in the book, need to unpack. In Job, therefore, it is important to make a distinction between the character of Job and the author of the book. We have analysed the structure of the book and become aware that we are reading what amounts to a play within a play. The fact that we have already encountered the patient Job of the prologue when we move on to the rebellious character of the dialogues leaves us with a feeling of suspended disbelief. However, it is in this section that a real character appears for the first time.

As I have mentioned, it is often held that an older prose tale was taken over by a fourth-century author who saw the potential of a rather simple and unrealistic story for saying something more profound. Just as an uncomplaining stance might be a way of hiding an inner anger, the author of the dialogue felt that patience was not the whole picture of how people react to suffering. The patience thus gives way to protest when the author of the dialogue gets to work. The sentiments we hear in the mouth of the protesting Job may well represent the experience of the author. Yet we need to ask further if there is, in the very structure of what has been written down, a hint of what the author was trying to do in writing this literature. Presumably he was writing in a particular context for particular people, using particular techniques to put across what he wanted to say. So he cleverly worked the prologue and dialogue together until a real character suddenly emerges from the model character of the first two chapters. But more than this, by placing the prologue and epilogue around his own dialogue section, which is full of the anguish and protest of Job, he relativizes the prose section. He has made the prose tale seem rather trite and ironic by putting it in a new context. I like the idea that perhaps the author was being deliberately tongue-in-cheek or ironic when he broke the literary illusion of the prose tale and put in his own completely contradictory message. However, his techniques do not stop there. Let us now look at a device he uses in the dialogue section itself to get across his protest on a more subtle literary level.

We have seen that the book of Job is usually classified amongst the wisdom literature of the Old Testament. However, whilst the book of Proverbs upholds traditional doctrines such as those represented by the friends—for example, that the good prosper and the wicked are punished—Job provides a challenge to such ideas. As such it is on the edge of the wisdom literature, representing a new direction for wisdom or even breaking out of its bounds. In the dialogue section, Job keeps accusing the friends of 'false wisdom'. Whilst the friends think that God does work and act in predictable ways, Job speaks of God as being arbitrary and conforming to no real pattern of justice or predictable behaviour, moral or otherwise. It may be then that the author was a renegade wise man—one who saw the weaknesses of the wisdom line and chose to lash out against it. He was a person on the fringe, possibly ahead of his time. Or perhaps rather than being on the edge of one tradition, he was at the centre of a new one—a group of sceptics, rather like the Greek sceptics, who felt it their charge to challenge known and accepted categories in order to promote self-questioning and change. Such contexts are necessarily hypothetical, but they go some way to bringing the author to us as a real person.

Authors usually employ techniques to achieve the effect they want. These can be very subtle and pass unnoticed except by those who set out to analyse such things. Thomas Hardy, for example, in all his tragedies starts with one event which then unfolds throughout the rest of the book, imposing inevitable repercussions on the hero or heroine, repercussions which are inescapable, almost predestined. When one starts to analyse his novels this pattern becomes blindingly obvious, but if one is simply reading them for pleasure it tends to pass one by, as it properly should if the novel is absorbing and well-constructed. In a sense when the reader is not aware of the techniques with which the author is working this is a measure of the success of the work.

When an author is in the position of challenging accepted tradition it is most effective if he or she starts from within that tradition, from the point that people are familiar with, and then leads the reader away and on to a new track. Because we are all familiar with certain patterns and genres, it takes us by surprise if suddenly the patterns are changed. For example, if we were sending a business letter which began 'Dear Sir', we would be taken aback if it ended 'Love from'. We are conditioned into expecting certain patterns of behaviour in certain contexts in the same way. Similarly, the wise of Israel used clever techniques in order to get their message across. Sometimes they cited views with which they did not agree in order to be able to argue against them. We see this technique at work in the book of Ecclesiastes, where the author uses the method of qualifying trite assurances made by earlier religious teachers. He submits to a test all the facts and experience he has gathered together. He comes to believe that God is an indifferent creator, remote from human beings, and he accepts these findings with an air of resignation: 'Then I saw all the work of God, that man cannot find out the work that is done under the sun. However much man may toil in seeking, he will not find it out; even though a wise man claims to know, he cannot find it out' (Ecclesiastes 8:17). I believe that the author of Job also uses a clever technique to express his message of protest against the orthodoxy of his day—that of parody. Let us look more closely at this.

If I began a story with the phrase 'Once upon a time' and ended with 'happily ever after' you would expect me to be telling a fairy tale, on the basis of recognizing the forms I used. If I changed the accepted form a little, it would make the reader sit up and notice. If I said 'Once upon a split second' or ended 'and they were all miserable unto eternity' you might wonder what on earth I was doing but your interest would probably be caught. This author is doing a similar thing in taking forms which are familiar to everyone—in particular from the Psalms —and filling them with an unexpected content.

In the dialogue section Job sees God as an oppressive presence. The author in fact conveys this by having Job speak in the very words that would have been used in the Psalms to praise God for his enduring faithfulness to human beings, but in order to convey the opposite of the traditional content. So, for example, in Psalm 8:4 the psalmist says 'What is man that thou art mindful of him, and the son of man that thou dost care for him?' The psalmist expresses awe at the favour God shows to human beings in his creation, and praises his majesty and his name. Job, however, turns this on its head: 'What is man, that thou dost make so much of him, and that thou dost set thy mind upon him, dost visit him every morning, and test him every moment?' (7:17–18). Here God is oppressive to Job for Job cannot get away from him. Job is tormented by God and just wants to be left alone. Furthermore, rather than seeing human beings as the apex of God's creative act, as the psalm does, Job sees humanity in more mundane terms as 'full of trouble' (Job 14:1).

Let us look at a few more examples of this. In the Psalms, death is usually seen as undesirable, often a sign of God's wrath. The plea is for God to look with favour and prevent sudden death or misfortune (e.g. Psalm 88:4–5). In Job death is longed for—death rather than God's favour would be the only release for Job from his present misery (3:11, 13, 21). Another example closely related to this is when Job pleads for death and longs for a place where he might escape from God: 'O that I might have my request, and that God would grant my desire; that it would please God to crush me, that he would let loose his hand and cut me off! This would be my consolation; I would even exult in pain unsparing; for I have not denied the words of the Holy One' (6:8–10). Usually in the Psalms the desire is to flee from the elements or from other people so that God can more easily be found (e.g. Psalm 55:6–8). A third example is in chapter 9:5–10, which appears to be a hymnic description of God's creative power, as one might find for example in Psalm 104. But instead of praising the wonder of creation, these descriptions in Job are reproaches against the God whose actions are unpredictable: 'He who removes mountains, and they know it not, when he overturns them in his anger'. Later in chapter 9 (25–28) instead of finding that he is troubled when he tries to forget God (as Jeremiah was in Jeremiah 20:9), Job is troubled when he tries to forget his suffering. In chapter 10, once again Job expresses a sentiment that is the opposite from what is expected. Usually the all-seeing eye of God is something to be praised (e.g. Psalm 139:7–8) but Job complains that he cannot escape from God—God seeks him out without telling him why. Job asks, 'Let me know why thou dost contend against me' (10:2). God is everywhere—he cannot escape from his presence or from his care: He begs God to 'Let me alone, that I may find a little comfort before I go whence I shall not return, to the land of gloom and deep darkness' (10:20–21). God has become for Job an oppressive presence.

This subtle technique by the author of the dialogue is found throughout that section and represents the turning of traditional forms and modes of thought on their head. I suggest that this technique can be likened to parody, which involves using other genres improperly to send up the original. This is used by the earliest masters of English literature. Chaucer, for example, in his *Tale of Sir Thopas,* parodies both the form and the content of the English romances of his day, including the romances of Bevis of Hampton and Guy of Warwick (whom he mentions in the tale). Sir Thopas can be appreciated fully only by a reader well versed in the clichés of the genre of popular romance—something that would pass most of us by today, no doubt. Sir Thopas exaggerates the events of popular romances to such an extent that they are ridiculed and the characters made to look comic and ridiculous.

Let us just look at a few more examples of this parodying technique in the dialogue of Job. Job 2:7–9 parodies a traditional form of praise to God as creator. The traditional line is that nature itself witnesses to the glory of God—in Job, nature witnesses to God's actions in the same way, but here God's actions are negative as they involve the misfortune inflicted on Job. The chapter goes on to see God's power as destructive, again reversing the positive praise of God found in psalms such as 107. Job complains, 'He deprives of speech those who are trusted, and takes away the discernment of the elders' (12:20). God is accused of working against human efforts to succeed in life. In chapter 13 Job goes back to the idea of wanting to be free from God. Unlike psalms which long to see God's face (e.g. Psalm 27:4), Job hides himself from God's face and asks to be left alone. He asks God to 'withdraw thy hand far from me' (13:21). How often do we, like Job, feel that we want just to run away into a corner and shut out the rest of the world? In chapter 14 Job pleads with God to leave man alone: 'Look away from him and desist, that he may enjoy, like a hireling, his day' (14:6). This parodies passages in the Psalms (e.g. Psalm 55:6–7) where the psalmist wishes to flee from his enemies—Job goes a step further in wanting to escape from God himself. Later in chapter 14 Job thinks that it would be good to go away from God but only for a while. He would wish to be recognized by God afresh when he had stopped being angry with him. He suggests that God hide him in Sheol—the land of the dead—and then restore him, but the catch is that, according to Hebrew thought, after death no such restoration to communion with God is possible. So Job is in fact asking for an impossibility here.

In a book called *The Pooh Perplex,* Frederick C. Crews takes a familiar, lovable bear and turns him into the subject of literary analysis. In the manner of literary critics who, as with Hardy, seek to analyse every aspect of the literary structure of a book and every aspect of the characters contained in it, Crews subjects Pooh to such a test. So he has chapters on the hierarchy of heroism in Pooh, notations on the hums of Pooh, the sacramental meaning of Pooh and so on. It soon becomes apparent, of course, that Crews is having us on. He has applied to a book not normally the subject of such analysis, an examination that is soon revealed to be 'over the top'. The book is in fact heavily ironic and is providing a parody of real books of this nature. Parody is a genre that feeds off others in that it plays on known poems, plays, phrases and traditions, and turns the content around, often for comic or ironic effect. Dr Johnson defined parody as 'a kind of writing in which the words of an author or his thoughts are taken and by a slight change adapted to some new purpose'. D. MacDonald, in the description I cited at the beginning of this chapter, provides us with another style of definition of the word: 'Parody is making new wine that tastes like the old but has a slightly lethal effect'.

I suggest that the new purpose of the author of Job when he added his inner story to the older one was to stimulate his hearers or readers into seeing that the traditional ideas were open to challenge and change. This was the result of his suffering and his protest—the realization that there was a need to subvert and to challenge the received tradition. By using the technique of parody—of using traditional forms in a fresh way—the author gets this across on the level of form as well as content. Let us look at a final few examples from the dialogue section. I mentioned in the first chapter the natural human tendency to remain hopeful in the face of misfortune. Job, in contrast to Psalms which also contain this feeling of hope, borne of trust in God, attacks this and accuses God directly of destroying the 'hope of man' (14:19). Again God is usually perceived in the Psalms as giving people the will to live, as providing them with the meaning in their lives that gives them the strength to go on. Psalm 94:18–19, for example, states, 'When I thought, "My foot slips", thy steadfast love, O Lord, held me up. When the cares of my heart are many, thy consolations cheer my soul'. Job says, however, 'God has worn me out' (16:7), 'He has torn me in his wrath, and hated me' (16:9) and 'I was at ease, and he broke me asunder' (16:12). Job is not a happy man.

How often, when emotional and upset, does one promote a point of view and then find oneself being contradictory? We have seen how fervently Job desires to flee from God's presence, but later in the dialogue, when he decides that he wishes to make a legal case against God, he starts complaining about God's absence: 'Behold I go forward, but he is not there; and backward, but I cannot perceive him; on the left hand I seek him, but I cannot behold him; I turn to the right hand, but I cannot see him' (Job 23:8–9). He wants it both ways. This contrasts with Psalms (e.g. 23) where God's presence is a constant, guiding power. Furthermore God's power is generally seen as a source of wonder and of comfort, but not by Job—he is frightened by God's power. In chapter 26 the author gets this across by using the traditional form of a hymn in praise of God's power, but to express its frightening rather than its more praiseworthy nature.

The dialogue gradually builds up to a climax, with Job laying his case before God and challenging him to a response. The climax to the entire book then comes when God actually appears to make some response to Job. And yet at this point too the author is tongue-in-cheek again. It is clear, even on a superficial reading, that God's words do not really answer the questions Job has been posing. Rather as Job's sentiments turn previous traditional stances on their head, so God in the speeches asks questions and makes statements regarding his work in creation that silence Job. And even then the irony still continues when, despite not receiving a satisfactory answer to his questions—although God's presence itself at least provides some response—Job nevertheless humbles himself and repents in dust and ashes. Again this could be seen as rather a non-sequitur. The author is perhaps teasing his readers and by that method leading them to ask more profound questions. Or perhaps the author is simply making the point that there are no answers to the questions raised. There is no answer to innocent suffering except that God's purposes are greater than ours. There is no answer to how God behaves except to stress his power and his arbitrariness. I shall go on to explore how there is no one answer to suffering but potentially a number. More important to stress here is that both Job the character and the author of Job are, on the levels of content and literary artistry, staging a protest against God and against traditional ideas about just rewards and the reasons for suffering. The final irony by the author is to have successfully overturned the idea that rewards and punishments are allocated in a manner that is fair, and then to retain the epilogue to the original story which seems to contradict all that has just been said by rewarding Job with a new set of children and twice as many animals as he had before.

So, the author had the courage of his convictions to overturn accepted literary forms of his day in order to shock his hearers or readers into questioning their own convictions. We have seen how the author's protest is put across on a subtle level in the techniques used, and how the book has been structured in a deliberately ironic way. In looking at examples of the parodying technique of this author we have seen the subtlety of the work and yet have also had the chance to look more closely at the sentiments of the suffering Job along the way. We shall look at Job's protest in more depth in the next chapter. It is clear that questioning leads to change or at least to a more profound addressing of the issues. This is the way the author makes his protest. He has Job the real character trying to rationalize and then betraying his emotion by swinging between extremes. Finally he grows through the suffering to have a firm idea of what appeal he wants to make to God. Job has the courage of his convictions and dares to doubt God. This is radical indeed.

6

Job the Rebel

Behold, I cry out, 'Violence!' but I am not answered;
I call aloud, but there is no justice.
He has walled up my way, so that I cannot pass,
and he has set darkness upon my paths.

Job 19:7–8

O Lord, thou hast deceived me, and I was deceived;
thou art stronger than I, and thou hast prevailed.
I have become a laughingstock all the day;
every one mocks me.

Jeremiah 20:7

I t is a striking fact that, contrary to the way many perceive the Bible, there is within its pages an acknowledgement that there is a place for shaking a fist at God and being angry. Somehow through the protest some kind of clarity often emerges, just as often through suffering itself some good can come—some fresh impetus, some fresh hope. The anger and protest are important for airing emotion and for the process of rationalizing, and ultimately for the process of acceptance. Realization of the unfairness of life cannot be reached without much anguish. Suffering leads us to question ourselves, God and other people. But it often leads to change and growth. Here too out of the questioning of old ideas comes the freshness of a new idea. It is the protesting spirit that questions traditional values and promotes the growth of fresh movements both in religion and in the wider world.

At the start of this chapter we have two cries of protest against God, one from Job and one from Jeremiah. Jeremiah is often compared to Job because of the similar sentiments he felt when suffering as a result of trying to preach God's message to people who did not want to hear it. He lived through the events that led to Israel's exile. He was in Jerusalem and had the task of proclaiming God's message of judgement to the nation. He found this task a great source of anguish, and it is his feelings on this that are explored in the 'Confessions'

(Jeremiah 11:18–12:6; 15:10–21; 17:14–18; 18:19–23; 20:7–12; and 20:14–18).

Rather like those who stand on soap boxes on Speakers' Corner in Hyde Park, shouting and pouring their heart out to a few uninterested bystanders, Jeremiah felt the full impact of the frustration that brought. He finds vent for his anger against God, rather as Job did. He accuses God of deceiving him—he had thought he was divinely commissioned to speak God's word to the people and then he finds that no one wants to hear. He asks, 'Why is my pain unceasing, my wound incurable, refusing to be healed? Wilt thou be to me like a deceitful brook, like waters that fail?' (15:18). Why then did God call him to prophesy in the first place? He asks such questions but receives no answer. There are many examples of people unrecognized in their own lifetime—musicians, artists, writers, politicians—who might well have asked why they were given such gifts and such a desire to express themselves but were shunned by their contemporaries. Such was Camille Claudel. She was a sculptor of immense talent, but she lived under the shadow of Auguste Rodin, another sculptor who did become famous in his own lifetime. Her work remained unrecognized except by a few—that few including Rodin himself, with whom she had a love affair. She gradually became disillusioned and unable to cope with her solitude and despair, and ended up being put into a lunatic asylum for the remaining thirty years of her life. Jeremiah's life was made miserable by having to be God's prophet—he was shunned and persecuted. He laments and bewails his lot in life from which he cannot escape. With hindsight we might look back and see Jeremiah as a figure of great importance for his time—good came out of the suffering eventually—but that was not how it seemed to him.

Job's protest is also to God whom he blames for his suffering. We have seen that throughout the dialogue Job is really addressing God rather than the friends, since the friends are not to blame, but are simply trying to help. Whilst we might ask why Job needs to blame God in this way and question whether he is right to do so, we have to acknowledge that blaming is an important part of the acceptance process. It is also part of the protest. Blaming someone else always makes us feel better as it is part of human nature not to want to take the blame but to pass it on to someone else or on to an institution—the government, the police, the education system, the legal system or, for some, on to God. We do not like having to face up to the fact that a great deal of the time it is we ourselves who are responsible. Job and Jeremiah can't find anyone else to blame except God, having decided that things are not fair and that the only one who can make things fair is him. Since he doesn't appear to be acting justly, he must be to blame. So Jeremiah appeals to God's justice and asks him to give evidence of behaving justly. He feels that he is a victim of injustice and so squarely lays the blame on God.

When a person is angry at the unfairness of a situation he or she starts to level all sorts of criticisms against the object of his or her anger. In the Old Testament that object is usually God. By now Job has also decided that God is arbitrary in his treatment of human beings, and he regards God as having turned against him. How often have we had the feeling that everyone and everything is against us? For many, God is a solace when other human beings appear to be hostile or hurtful, but what if God too appears to be absent or powerless or cruel? This brings us back to the experience of those in the Holocaust. We saw how in such a situation some people lost their faith whilst others protested at God but could not give up their faith in him, and in the end felt strengthened by that faith. For both Jeremiah and Job giving up on God completely was not an option. They stayed within the framework of belief in God even though they staged a protest against God. In fact the very belief that their affliction was from God made their pains harder to bear.

Job talks of God's arrows as having been fired at him—poisoned arrows which can only bring evil. He openly charges God with being his tormentor. He sees God's constant attention to him as oppressive. God guards him like the sea monster (7:12) and scares him with terrifying visions (7:13–14). All Job wants is to be left alone, and he asks why puny man should be given such attention by God (7:17). If he has indeed sinned why should God even mind, why should he be so concerned? This is the main theme of his first speech in chapters 6 and 7. In his second speech he goes on to protest about the fact that one cannot contend with God as an equal. It is no use arguing with God: God can use his power to overwhelm humans by posing unanswerable questions (as in fact he does later on in the book). God always comes off best and human beings have no power against him. This is rather like that feeling of helplessness in the face of natural disaster—the power of the earthquake, flood or tornado is such that human beings are swept out of existence in its path. The power is so terrifying that we can do nothing to prevent the inevitable happening. Despite attempts to construct technical equipment to predict the first rumblings of an earthquake, the whole thing happens so quickly that one wonders if there is really any chance of combating its effect. Job and Jeremiah perceive God as the creator and hence the one who holds that kind of power in his grasp, and in the face of that power they feel completely helpless and small.

Both Job and Jeremiah see their confrontation with God very much in legal terms. As God sets the standard of justice in the first place, there is no higher court to which appeal can be made against his decisions: God is both the opposition and the judge. God is therefore accused of not governing the world in a moral way. But if God is all power and no morals, what can man do in arguing with him?—God is too mighty and man too feeble to stand up to him. Job is on a losing wicket, the odds are stacked against him.

One often feels when mistreated that one needs to take the matter further. Sometimes an argument with the wrongdoer seems justified. At other times an argument clears the air— through argument we come to hear the views of others and eventually we effect healing. This is a positive result, but more often than not it is negative—if the argument remains unresolved then it leads to conflict. Arguments can turn nasty, sometimes to such an extent that appeal to a higher court is required. We need to have a system of law that maintains society in an ordered way and yet we all know that even that is not foolproof. Innocent people have been sent to the gallows, and police and lawyers are not always honest and fair. Yet somehow the presence of such a system gives us stability. What, however, if we could no longer trust in the system? What if we knew that the very heart of it was rotten and that however hard we tried we were not going to get a fair trial? That is the kind of thing Job feels—his very court of appeal (God) is inflicting the unjust suffering. So he has no court any more. No one can judge his innocence fairly since God is setting the rules and meting out the punishment. God is all-powerful and is abusing his position, so Job launches a searing attack upon God's irresponsible and unjust power-mongering. He is arbitrary and vents his wrath upon anyone he pleases. Because of his power, a human being has no chance of even facing God, let alone answering him. Job says, 'Though I am innocent, my own mouth would condemn me; though I am blameless, he would prove me perverse' (9:20).

God causes everything to be, therefore it is assumed that he is to blame for everything. Job even accuses God of causing him to speak such bitter words: 'He will not let me get my breath, but fills me with bitterness' (9:18) and, of course, he is to blame for all wickedness on the earth: 'The earth is given in to the hand of the wicked; he covers the faces of its judges—if it is not he, who then is it?' (9:24). Jeremiah persistently asks the same question, 'Why does the way of the wicked prosper? Why do all who are treacherous thrive?' (12:1b). Today we might not want to speak in terms of 'good' and 'wicked' people—for who are we to make such a judgement on others? However, we often feel that rewards, material for example, are not fairly meted out. Our world is such that certain activities are rewarded much more highly than others—a pop star, for instance, will enjoy international acclaim and high material rewards; a professor, on the other hand, will also enjoy international acclaim but be paid a pittance by comparison.

Situations sometimes arise in which someone we thought we could trust—our best friend perhaps—does something to shatter our trust. We suddenly feel let down, shunned, our trust abused. Things will never be the same again, even if we find it in our hearts to forgive. Job feels that of God—he was once the one Job relied on, now he has turned nasty. He accuses God of mocking when disaster strikes, almost enjoying it. Job begins to wonder whether God follows the same system of justice as human beings, but since that human system is the only one he can understand he ends up deciding that God must know of his innocence. He feels that he needs an umpire to justify him to God—God, his protector, who is now his prison warder. Jeremiah feels similarly that God is aware of the injustices befalling him and does nothing about it. Why does God refuse to act? he asks. Can God in the end be relied upon?

In the biblical tradition there is much praise to God as creator, feeling creation to be a wonderful gift from God—Psalm 104, for example:

> O Lord my God, thou art very great! Thou art clothed with honour and majesty, who coverest thyself with light as with a garment, who hast stretched out the heavens like a tent, who hast laid the beams of thy chambers on the waters, who makest the clouds thy chariot, who ridest on the wings of the wind, who makest the winds thy messengers, fire and flame thy ministers.
>
> Psalm 104:1–4

In his third speech Job seems to start by praising God as creator but then it is clear that he is also blaming God for all the bad things in nature. God acts as capriciously and arbitrarily in nature as in his dealings with man so there is no point trying to find patterns in nature that can be predicted—nothing is predictable and God is answerable to no one: 'Behold, he snatches away; who can hinder him? Who will say to him, "What doest thou?"' (Job 9:12).

An important part of human life is to feel respected and valued by others. Often when we suffer at the hands of someone else, or if we suffer illness or disaster, there is a feeling of losing status within the community. People were kind at first, but are they not becoming rather tired of hearing about our misfor-

tunes? Perhaps people feel embarrassed by the misfortune of
others and so stay away not wanting to get involved. Perhaps
people misunderstand what has really been going on and are
suspicious and untrusting of us, and we are unable to be heard
for what we are. Jeremiah feels mocked by others. He says, 'I
have become a laughingstock all the day; every one mocks me'
(20:7). Job feels not only mocked by others but also by God.
God, he claims, reverses human fortunes, mocking the good in
man and making fun of man's attempts to serve him. Job uses
the example of the rise and fall of nations, which does not appear to be governed by any moral principle. I am reminded of
the story of Jonah where God's restoration of the nation of
Nineveh seems to be on a whim and largely arbitrary. Jonah
too is a character who dares to challenge God—he tells God
that by deciding to forgive the Ninevites he has wasted Jonah's
time! Job accuses God of arbitrariness. In chapter 13 Job pleads
with God for an opportunity to state his case—he needs a personal answer: 'But I would speak to the Almighty, and I desire
to argue my case with God' (13:3). God must explain himself
for his apparently arbitrary action.

A common reaction to misfortune is to wish something
hadn't happened and try to imagine what life was like before it
happened. When a relationship has gone wrong and two people
decide to part, it is hard to recapture what it has once been like.
We either over-idealize the way it used to be or we find we cannot think ourselves back into such feelings again. We can see
Job still longing to retain his old idea of God and his old fellowship with God from which he feels cut off. His suffering is
only evidence of his abandonment by God. He believes that
God will one day long for his fellowship—surely God too is
suffering from the breakdown of this relationship—and yet the

evidence points in the opposite direction. Job claims that God destroys his hopes for renewal of the relationship.

In the second cycle of speeches Job gets more heated. He perceives God to have abandoned him and caused others to oppose him. God is compared to a wild beast—'He has torn me in his wrath, and hated me; he has gnashed his teeth at me; my adversary sharpens his eyes against me' (16:9). He feels that others are massed against him, gaping at him and abusing him. He feels that God has cast him into the hands of the wicked and broken him. Such an attack was completely unexpected: 'I was at ease, and he broke me asunder; he seized me by the neck and dashed me to pieces' (16:12). However God has treated him, he is his only witness and to him Job must appeal. Job begs that his rights be maintained. He changes his stance here, and rather than bewailing the fact that there is no one to whom he might appeal to stand between him and God, he now begs God nevertheless to take up his case.

One aspect of intense suffering is a preoccupation with death. When a person has a terminal illness, for example, there is a strong feeling that death must be put off as long as possible— there are too many things one wanted to achieve, one is too young to die. But then, when the disease takes hold, death is eventually a release, almost a welcome guest. Job is preoccupied with the thought that if he dies he will not be able to make his case to God. He is sure that death is imminent and is worried that if he dies he will never be vindicated. He longs for death as a release from suffering but is worried that if he dies it will be too late. Like Jeremiah when he felt mocked and a laughingstock, Job bewails the fact that his friends now scorn him and have become his accusers, but he later accuses God of making the friends not understand him. 'Since thou hast closed their minds to understanding, therefore thou wilt not let them triumph' (17:4)—it is all God's fault! He threatens the friends saying that one day their children will suffer for their heartlessness. He reminds them that they are just as likely to be judged as he is. But generally he blames God—'Know then that God has put me in the wrong and closed his net about me' (19:6). As a hunter deals with animals, God has now stripped Job of the honourable reputation he once enjoyed.

Some days everything is wrong, on others all is right with the world. Some days one feels positive about life, about relationships, about work, on other days it would be good just to give the whole lot up. Job's feelings fluctuate in this way. He has moments of more positive thought, such as in 19:26 when he asserts that one day, possibly after death, God will vindicate him and Job will be aware of his vindication. At this thought Job's heart faints within him—he is overcome by the thought, which seems too wonderful to be true. Here we can clearly see the conflict within Job: he has always loved and served God, and in this moment of optimism he wants all to be right again and to put aside his despair. It is rather like waking from a dream—sometimes when something is on one's mind it is forgotten in sleep and one dreams pleasant thoughts. Then one wakes up...and nothing has changed, one is back to despair again.

Job comes back to the problem of the prosperity of the wicked in this cycle of speeches—they prosper and they see their children prosper. There is no punishment in the next generation either. Job protests that it would be no justice for a person to sin and his children to suffer for it rather than him. The sinner himself should be corrected and disciplined. Job questions anyway whether a man takes an interest in the affairs of his family once he is dead. Death levels all—the wicked man dies at ease and in prosperity, and the good man dies in bitterness, but the same fate is meted out to both and in the grave both bodies rot away. This is not just abstract theorizing, it is the cry of an anguished person trying to know something about a God who seems to be doing the opposite of what is expected of him.

One of the reactions to the Holocaust was the feeling that God was absent or at least hidden. This is a common feeling amongst those who suffer—that they have been abandoned, that no one understands or cares, even sometimes God. In the third cycle of speeches, Job expresses the desire to find God and come to his dwelling, and he is sure that God will give him a fair hearing rather than simply overwhelming him by his power. Again this is a more positive moment—God will allow an upright man to reason with him and he will be for ever acquitted by his judge (23:7). Job is annoyed by the certainty of the friends that they know God's ways and that God is just. But then Job realizes that God cannot be found in this way, he is hidden from Job. He decides that this relationship is rather one-sided—God knows where he is, what he is thinking, what he is doing, but Job does not know God's dwelling place and he cannot understand what he is doing. This is the opposite of the sentiments expressed earlier by Job that he felt hemmed in by God. Now God cannot be found and all that hems him in is darkness—in chapter 23 Job thinks of God's inscrutability and is frightened 'for I am hemmed in by darkness, and thick darkness covers my face' (23:17).

God does not only seem to be hidden but he is inactive. Job accuses God of inactivity in the face of human oppression and injustice since he appears to take no notice of the poor, the suffering, the godly, nor even of the wicked. Why doesn't God let those who follow him see that he brings such wickedness to judgement? Again Job enumerates the evil deeds of humans which go unpunished, again he criticizes the friends for thinking they have all the answers, accusing them of false wisdom. In chapter 27 Job repeats that God has wronged him and made his soul bitter. Yet he swears an oath by this same God—a strange contradiction. Here he is determined to hold on to truth, to righteousness and to his integrity whatever the friends say: 'As long as my breath is in me, and the spirit of God is in my nostrils; my lips will not speak falsehood, and my tongue will not utter deceit' (27:34).

At the heart of Job's protest then is his protest against God, and in his anger and despair he says many radical things against him. Yet God is the one he has loved and followed, and we find glimpses of longing for the certainty that he had before and longing for that relationship to be restored. It is clear that Job's protest contains many different arguments, many of which are self-contradictory.

It seems to me to be a keynote of that feeling of anger and helplessness which suffering often engenders, that we are full of contradictions. Different sentiments come to the fore at different stages and times during the process of rationalization and acceptance. This is certainly true of Job, who keeps contradicting himself. Consistently we find the themes of the arbitrariness and injustice of God in Job's speeches, and yet there is also the feeling that God will be just and Job will be vindicated at some stage. Job says that God may have his own system of justice of which human beings know nothing, and therefore that humans are floundering around in the dark, and yet this system is all that he knows and ultimately he believes that God will hear him. There is a profound feeling of unfairness but it is tempered by the thought that some kind of fair system will come into play eventually. Perhaps we have here the origin of ideas about the afterlife—if there are no just rewards in this life then surely they will occur in the life hereafter…?

In Job we have another contradiction. God is seen now to have turned against Job and become his tormentor. There is the inference that he enjoys inflicting suffering or does so for fun. Job refuses to believe in a just God any longer, and yet there is the plea for mercy, the hope that God will one day long for Job's fellowship. The anger is mixed with the anguish. Sometimes there is the feeling that God's attention to Job is oppressive yet at other times God cannot be found, and Job sees it as unfair that God knows where Job is whilst he cannot find God. Job does not extol God's greatness, but bewails the fact that God is not an equal to be contended with fairly, since he can overwhelm with his more abundant power and knowledge, which he uses to guarantee that he always comes off best. Who is holding God to account? Why doesn't God explain himself? Why is God breaking the will of the faithful and destroying their hopes? All Job ends up with is more questions and fewer answers. But somehow his position has moved throughout the dialogue and he has become more certain. He has formulated his strongest arguments and reduced them to a plea for God to appear to justify himself. This, in the end, is the only answer that will satisfy Job. He also ends his final speech on a note of optimism, of strength, of holding on to his integrity. He has almost acquired the stature of a tragic hero. His faith might well be said to have been strengthened by this experience—not that that is in itself a good reason for suffering. In the way he leaves the arguments of the friends behind, Job seems to be moving on to a deeper plane and asking more profound questions. The importance of anger and protest in life comes to the fore here. Rightly or wrongly it makes us feel a lot better! It helps us to formulate what we really feel to be important. It leads us to question other people and to question God. More significantly, if often leads to change and growth—out of the questioning of old ideas comes the freshness of new ones.

So, challenge often leads to change and growth, and although it may cause much anger and anguish on the way, the outcome is often positive. We have seen the anguish caused to Jeremiah by the task he has to do, but in the end he could not give up on God. He tries to shut God out of his life but fails: 'If I say, "I will not mention him, or speak any more in his name", there is in my heart as it were a burning fire shut up in my bones, and I am weary with holding it in, and I cannot' (Jeremiah 20:9). Other prophets of Israel, in similar vein to Job, questioned the accepted assumptions of their day in order to express something new. Amos, for example, questioned the attitude of the people towards their religious practices, towards their treatment of each other and towards God. Amos' questioning may well have been part of his own struggle to come to terms with his identity as a prophet of God, and to communicate this to his contemporaries. It is clear that faith has to be challenged and attitudes need to change in order that faith can survive. The mistake of the friends is that they are unprepared to change their stance in the light of new evidence; rather they condemn Job for the experience he has that makes him differ from them in his opinions. Job, on the other hand, is prepared to overthrow all he had formerly believed and to face the chaos of starting afresh.

There are some biblical characters who not only dare to stand up to God as Job and Jeremiah did in order to vent their feelings, but who actually persuade him to change his mind. This is a strand of thought that later editors of the Old Testament found rather embarrassing since it suggested a limitation of God's power. Still it is there and the positive aspect of it is that it suggests that since God too is in relationship with humankind, he can be persuaded to change his mind. This might well be related to the power of prayer—God is listening and he makes his response in his own time. People clearly believed that God's mind could be changed, and saw him as able to be argued with freely. Moses is one such character who is not afraid to voice objections to God's purposes and intentions. In Exodus 32 Moses says to God, 'Turn from thy fierce wrath and repent of this evil against thy people'. This happens at the point when God is about to destroy Israel for making a golden calf. It is a bold plea which we find answered in these words, 'and the Lord repented of the evil which he thought to do to his people'. Moses appeals to two things, God's name or reputation and his past action which becomes a commitment for future action. We find these arguments frequently used in the Psalms to beg God to act—in Psalm 25:11, for example, the psalmist says: 'For thy name's sake, O Lord, pardon my guilt, for it is great', and in Psalm 22:4, 'In thee our fathers trusted; they trusted, and thou didst deliver them. To thee they cried, and were saved; in thee they trusted, and were not disappointed'. These are arguments we might well use whilst contending with God over the unfairness of human suffering—first, the appeal to God's reputation: if God wants us to believe in him, why does he not act in a way that would make it easy? There is also the thought that whilst God acts in this way, others will not be led to believe. Believers have a hard time persuading others that God makes any difference to their lives, especially when suffering occurs. Second, the appeal to God's action in the past: we prospered in the past, so why not now? Why doesn't God act in a way that is consistent?

We have seen Job and Jeremiah appeal to God's consistency. Abraham also does this in Genesis 18 when he protests against God's decree that Sodom should be destroyed. He asks, 'Shall not the Judge of all the earth do right?' He dares to suggest to God that the presence of just a few righteous people in the place ought to count for something in God's eyes. He makes a good point in dialogue with God, and so God changes his mind. His appeal is that God must remain true to his moral nature. Unlike Job, who begins to wonder if God's system of justice is the same as ours, Abraham presupposes that God does act in an understandable and morally justifiable way. Job wants to believe that too, but his experience is making him question it. Abraham, however, is able to trust God and yet question him at one and the same time. Perhaps we can draw a slightly different conclusion from Abraham's case: we have no need to abandon our belief in a God whose nature we know when things go wrong or seem to be incomprehensible. God's purposes may be hidden, they may appear to be nonsensical, but there is nothing to stop us from having a good argument with him. Abraham's questioning is fairly tame compared to that of Job, but the fact that he is able to question is an important point— he can challenge God and try to change the status quo, and the fact that God is so challenged implies a relationship and not a dictatorship.

We have seen the different stages through which Job has moved in the course of the dialogue. These represent different stages of working through his anguish and his protest at God. He profoundly questions traditional ideas about God, and he refutes established religious positions as represented by the friends. He feels at one and the same time positive and negative—he feels sceptical of the possibility of ever understanding anything, he feels pessimistic about the attempt to even try to understand, but something keeps him going and in the end maybe he has grown as a person and grown in his understanding even if he has not got all the answers. Job wages a protest against God's treatment of him and it seems that he is silenced, except for the existence of one verse (42:7) which states that God is angry with the friends because 'you have not spoken of me what is right, as my servant Job has'. Here it seems that Job's protest is being confirmed—Job was perhaps right to question. He grew in his faith through his suffering so that he no longer accepts pat answers such as the friends tried to give him. Perhaps, after all, we are not to feel so bad about shaking a fist at God—it seems that protest is all part of the suffering process.

Protest then is a legitimate response to suffering. It forms a small, yet important, part of the Old Testament tradition. Daring to question God is an important stage in our self-understanding. The different challenges posed to God raise some interesting options when we come to explore possible responses to suffering that we might make today.

7

Any Answers?

To be told so little—to such an end—and still,
finally, to be denied an explanation....

Tom Stoppard,
Rosencrantz and
Guildenstern Are Dead

The idea that life cannot be explained, that there are more questions than answers, and that human beings are floundering around trying to make sense of things that ultimately have no explanation was one that characterized the existentialist movement. We have been looking at the play *JB* which was written at this time. Here I quote from *Rosencrantz and Guildenstern Are Dead*, a powerful play by Tom Stoppard at the tail-end of the existentialist movement. In this play two figures are taken from the play *Hamlet*, and they are portrayed as waiting in the wings until they are 'on stage'. Only when they are in *Hamlet* do their lives have any direction, outside it they are living in a state of constant unknowing, of meaninglessness and lack of direction. Like the characters in Samuel Becket's existentialist play, *Waiting for Godot*, these two are waiting to discover something, they know not what, that will illuminate their lives. But in the end they never receive any explanation of what happens to them at the hands of others.

I have tried to show how the tradition of protesting against God is a biblical one and a legitimate response to suffering. Job is angry at God—he had the courage to doubt God and to blame him—and yet he never stopped trusting in him: 'I tell you God himself has put me in the wrong and drawn his net about me. If I shout "Violence" no one answers; if I appeal for help I get no justice'. Much of Job is about humankind's relationship to

God and vice versa. A theological profundity has entered the debate here which involves the whole question of the nature of the Godhead. It raises ultimate questions of the purpose of existence but via a different route to the one taken by the existentialists.

Rosencrantz did not get any answers, nor did Vladimir and Estragon in *Waiting for Godot*—they knew they were waiting for Godot and that he would save them, but they never knew who he was or when he was coming, and all they could do was continue to wait. However, in the book of Job, God does respond, although it is not in the way Job expects. So what is God's response? It is basically to ask questions, make a series of statements and provide no concrete answers. He asks Job where he was at creation: 'Where were you when I laid the foundation of the earth? Tell me, if you have understanding. Who determined its measurements—surely you know!' (38:4–5). The inference is that the whole scale on which God is working is greater than ours. He talks of his action in creation and in nature: 'Who has cleft a channel for the torrents of rain, and a way for the thunderbolt, to bring rain on a land where no man is, on the desert in which there is no man; to satisfy the waste and desolate land, and to make the ground put forth grass?' He overwhelms Job with a display of his knowledge and power. We might ask what kind of God we are being presented with here and how satisfactory this response is. It is clear that this picture of God is unlike others that we find in the Old Testament. The more usual reference is to God's many acts in history on behalf of the people of Israel, not exclusively to his works in creation. We might ask why the author of Job falls back on this concept of God's overwhelming power and ability to do whatever he likes. Is it in order to draw a complete contrast between the all-knowing supremacy of God and man's ignorance and limited knowledge? It implies that there is no answer to the question why suffering has been imposed upon humankind. It also suggests that, despite his power, God could not create the kind of world we live in, with human beings having intelligence and free choice, without pain and suffering being a constituent part of their lives.

Job repents. He says first, 'Behold, I am of small account; what shall I answer thee? I lay my hand on my mouth' (40:4), and second, 'I have uttered what I did not understand...I had heard of thee by the hearing of the ear but now my eye sees thee; therefore I despise myself and repent in dust and ashes' (42:3, 5–6). It seems that somehow he has found some kind of answer although it is not clear precisely what that is. Is he simply overwhelmed by what God has to say? Does he fully accept that God is a distant creator who does things too great for us to comprehend and whose justice is greater than ours? Or is it simply the fact that God does at least appear for him enough to satisfy him?

The author of Psalm 73—who was troubled by the fact that ungodly people and blasphemers of God prospered and suffered no pain or misfortune—when he went into the sanctuary of God, suddenly saw things clearly and in perspective: 'But when I thought how to understand this, it seemed to me a wearisome task; until I went into the sanctuary of God; then I perceived their end'. He saw that God's judgement was in the end just as he had always believed it to be. He also saw that God was guiding and upholding him: 'For me it is good to be near God; I have made the Lord God my refuge, that I may tell of all thy works'. There seems to be something in beholding the presence of God that is comforting. The questioning is, perhaps only temporarily, superseded by a greater feeling of serenity, strength and peace in bearing the particular difficulty. It is often an answer to suffering that there is no spoken answer but God is alongside in the suffering, helping one to bear it, helping one to put it to good effect.

If God is a distant creator, however, how can we relate to him? How do we know what his system of justice is? How can we respond? Is he just an unknowable tyrant who plays with human beings for sport? We might well get this impression from the wager in the prologue of Job. At the heart of Job's plea was the desire for justice. We have seen how he phrases it as a legal appeal: 'Oh that I knew where I might find him, that I might come even to his seat! I would lay my case before him and fill my mouth with arguments. I would learn what he would answer me, and understand what he would say to me' (23:3–5). Job is here appealing to God's consistency. He perceived that at the heart of his faith was the justice of God and that God could not act other than in a consistent way. The fact that God appears at least confirms a certain consistency, although Job never receives an answer to why he has suffered in this way nor does he receive any response to his rational arguments. If God has given us reason, then why are we not being allowed to use it? What is the nature of Job's repentance—is it rational? Perhaps we are being told here that in relationship with God, the rational is transcended. We are not going to find instant answers but God is there for us all the same.

If God is arbitrary then we need to abandon all ideas of God having a plan. It would be an inconceivable idea that God would deliberately select some people to suffer. I suppose one could argue that most suffering is inflicted by human beings on other human beings, and when God sees human beings doing these things to each other, presumably he suffers too. Perhaps a better answer is that much suffering is caused by unchanging laws of nature and is therefore outside God's control, since he lets nature tick according to its own clock. That is all very well, but then what about miracles? God is seen to overturn nature in miracles, why not then at other times? God is all-powerful, yes, but perhaps he is leaving us the space to have a choice between right and wrong, and in doing so he is opening up all sorts of possibilities of suffering.

One interesting part of the epilogue of Job that is often overlooked is Job's intercession for the friends. God vindicates Job by criticizing what the friends have said, and then Job intercedes for the friends who are seen to have said false things: 'The Lord said to Eliphaz the Temanite: "My wrath is kindled against you and against your two friends; for you have not spoken of me what is right, as my servant Job has. Now therefore take seven bulls and seven rams, and go to my servant Job, and offer up for yourselves a burnt offering; and my servant Job shall pray for you, for I will accept his prayer, not to deal with you according to your folly; for you have not spoken of me what is right, as my servant Job has" ' (42:7–8). Within the message of judgement on the friends there is an implicit message of forgiveness in Job's intercessory role. The friends held on to what they perceived to be true. Job did the same but his perception of God became very different from theirs. He is here atoning for them. We might tentatively draw a parallel with Jesus, who bore the sins of others in his suffering on the cross. Perhaps one way of overcoming suffering is to look outside oneself to others, without hope of reward but for its own sake. Perhaps we just have to accept that life is precarious and that God is not to blame for everything. We need to trust in him and gain strength from him. Job trusted God and never gave up his faith in him: 'Though he slay me, yet will I trust in him' (13:15 AV). Habakkuk echoes the sentiment: 'Though the fig tree do not blossom, nor fruit be on the vines, the produce of the olive fail and the fields yield no food, the flock be cut off from the fold and there be no herd in the stalls, yet I will rejoice in the Lord, I will joy in the God of my salvation' (3:17–18). Perhaps we are wrong to blame God and hold him responsible. We should be looking to making a better world, beginning with human beings. Job's protest sprang out of his pain and sense of injustice. It was part of his character to protest, to vent his anger, not at others (although the friends came in for a certain amount of criticism) but mainly at the situation he found himself in and for which he held God responsible. So we can find great relief by protesting—even at God—but perhaps we are wrong in the end to blame God. It is good to try to rationalize and think through the problems as Job did, but wrong to lay the blame on God or to think that there is always an answer. In today's world we know the answer to much that past generations would have attributed to God's action—we have increased medical knowledge so that we know what many of the causes of much physical and some mental pain are, and we can control pain to a great extent. We understand more about the human psyche and about the dynamics of human relationships. And yet we still have questions about our human experience that no amount of medical know-how or psychoanalysis can answer, and the answer to suffering is one of those.

It is clear that Job is a very human character who suffered just like us and yet who shook his fist at God and the world and finally came to some kind of reconciliation with God. We too may learn and grow through suffering and through challenging and protesting. We are open to the precariousness of life and we can only trust in God, ask him to give us the strength to cope, and try to look outside ourselves so that good can come out of situations of suffering. We noted at the start that, on balance, a feeling of hope and forward-looking prevails over wallowing in the depths of despair. Maybe we just have to accept what comes to us—not seeing misfortune as God's fault but rather as chance or misfortune in an imperfect world. But there is every reason why we should feel justified in shaking our fist at God a little—and at others—along the way.

We have by now asked many questions about suffering and seen the way many of them are raised and reacted to in the book of Job. We might try to order our thoughts concerning the possibility of rationalizing suffering by putting different solutions down in a list. It may be that none of these possibilities provides an answer for us, but some have more mileage than others. We may have to be content with a range of answers, if indeed they can be regarded as answers. They are perhaps to be seen rather as varying reactions. It strikes me that no one answer is given in Job. In the juxtaposition of different endings and in the raising of different issues without resolution, the author is perhaps airing various possibilities for the reader to evaluate.

1. We have just seen God's answer that his purposes are greater than ours. It is possible that there may be some higher purpose which we do not understand. We may come to understand it eventually, or we may never do so. It may be part of a greater mystery and incomprehensibility of the Godhead that we, with our human reason, can never ascertain. We might argue that this is rather an

unsatisfactory answer because if God is totally other from us, and totally incomprehensible according to any kinds of category we may try to think in, then how can we relate in any way to him? If he has revealed himself in history to us and has given us some idea of his nature in the past, then surely we can expect there to be some consistency and some possibility of interaction and mutual understanding.

2. Related to this is the idea Job toys with that God's justice is on a different level to ours. He uses this observation to question whether God is moral at all. It is sometimes asserted that God's justice is so much greater than ours or on a different plane, so that our attempts to fit his actions into a theory of just retribution are simply child's folly. This is the kind of response we get in God's speeches—he is working on such a different level that human beings are put in their place when they realize it. We might want to question this as a satisfactory answer.

3. The theory of just retribution is an age-old answer—as the friends maintain, Job must have sinned. There is often the idea that one transgression leads to a balancing misfortune, as if one has one's 'fair share' of each. We have come across this argument in the dialogue of Job, and in the end Job refuses to believe in such a pattern. Related to this is the idea that even though there are injustices in this life, all will be worked out in the next: in the afterlife, the good and wicked will get what they deserve. We might want to question the simplicity of this response.

4. One possible answer is that God is not so powerful after all—God has his limitations or has imposed limitations

upon himself. One of his limitations is the natural world itself and the fact that everything happens according to laws and rules of nature. The need for predictability in life is stressed, but in a world governed by laws, catastrophes such as earthquakes, floods and other natural disasters are bound to happen. This is the conclusion reached by Richard Harries in the article on 'Evidence for the love of God' that I cited earlier. Some scholars have argued that Job's repentance is rather tongue-in-cheek and that in fact, after God has spoken, he recognizes God's limitations.

5. Suffering is wholly to do with the evil of human beings, either that of the sufferer or of someone else. Humans make cars, trains or aeroplanes which will inevitably crash from time to time. Humans make nuclear warheads that fall into the wrong hands. Humans desire material goods and are prepared to go to excessive lengths to get them. Humans each want different things—they form groups, nations, ideologies that inevitably conflict and lead to wars. The world is an imperfect place when it is filled with human beings, and we simply have to accept that fact.

6. Related to 5 is the idea that humans are fallen and sinful. God gave humanity a choice, he gave humans free will and they chose evil. All God can now do is try to help to create good out of the evil that inevitably exists. C. S. Lewis took this line in *The Problem of Pain*. We might ask why God created such a world. Maybe that is a non-question since we do not know all the creative options and conditions that God had before him. Maybe God had no choice. Or maybe he chose to allow humans to exercise free will and this is the result.

7. Suffering is part of the learning process—both learning about yourself and other people. We looked at this in chapter 3. It is even said that you can't really know yourself until you have suffered. Even more, it is said that you can't really help others in their suffering if you have not suffered yourself. One might question these statements quite strongly. Suffering can lead to self-knowledge but is by no means the only route, and how often has the innocent remark of a child helped to ease the pain of a situation?

8. The soul of man reaches perfection through suffering. Somehow suffering represents a higher way, and through it purificatory atonement can be achieved. Again we looked at this in chapter 3 and found it to be an unrealistic reaction for most people. I am reminded of the saints and martyrs who embraced suffering and death with great readiness. It raises the question of whether alleviating pain is right or wrong—if pain is part of this suffering should it simply be borne?

9. Suffering is part of the human condition, part of what it is to be human. If one has not suffered one is not truly part of the human race. Suffering allows us to deepen our character, grow in maturity and reconsider our attitudes. God holds both good and evil in tension and we have to accept a share of each from him.

10. God is goodness but he has created man with the propensity to good or evil. He cannot prevent the suffering but he enables us to cope with it. He should not be blamed for our suffering, rather he shares in it. He shows his love to us and encourages us to accept it and to look outside ourselves to others. God suffers in and with the world.

God is with the victim and the sinner. Through suffering we often feel closer to God. God's love is at the centre— even if he and we are imperfect. Response to that love is what is needed, along with acceptance of the suffering and the will to carry on living with an eye to the needs of others as well as ourselves.

These answers or responses to suffering are not in any particular order, except that the response that I find most satisfactory is the last one, number 10. It seems to me that Job's mistake is to blame God as if God is to be held responsible. God has given us free will, and that involves trusting him but at the same time realizing that the world is imperfect and that human beings have the freedom to do evil to each other, and to do so with alarming regularity. It is to realize that accidents happen and that God is not to blame, but is suffering alongside us, helping us to go through the process of anguish, of protest and of eventual acceptance. As Job's story ends with his intercession on behalf of the friends, so we might overcome our own suffering by a spirit of forgiveness and by looking outside ourselves to others. I want in the final chapter to explore this answer in a Christian context. This is not to say that this kind of answer cannot arise in a Jewish or other religious context, but I think that putting it into a Christian framework is helpful at this stage. It may be alternatively that with Guildenstern in the play I cited at the beginning of this chapter you prefer to conclude that there are no answers, only questions....To have the courage to hold this position and work it through for yourself is perhaps the first stage of coming to a more profound understanding.

8

A Christian Response

Blow on the coal of the heart.
The candles in churches are out.
The lights have gone out in the sky.
Blow on the coal of the heart
And we'll see by and by…

A. MacLeish, JB

The story [of Job] does not solve the problem [of suffering]. There is no solution. But it points the way to an understanding sufficient for reasonable and heroic faith. There is further insight in the Christian doctrine of the Incarnation whereby God himself enters the world's suffering, and through it works the world's redemption. But the main purpose of religion, even of Christian religion, is not to give an intellectual answer to the most baffling of problems but to give inner strength and power to gain the victory over the trials which provoke the questionings. And that is far better.

From the introduction to a service based on Job
by Canon J. Bezzant

I have occasionally referred to parallels with Jesus or hinted at a Christian outlook but I have deliberately avoided bringing that too much into the discussion. By putting these thoughts at the end I do not want to imply that Christianity has all the answers. It often comes up with much the same answers as Judaism regarding suffering; however, in its belief in the redemptive suffering of Jesus Christ, Christianity inevitably provides a different perspective. It is important to remember that the book of Job is in the Hebrew Bible, the Christian Old Testament, and not in the New. One of my students once said to me he thought Job was so full of meaning for Christians today that it should be in the New Testament. Isn't the point, I replied, that it is in the Old and that it shows how much the Old Testament has to say to Christians today if only they would read it and learn from it? That however is another issue for another day....

I want to start with the character of Jesus. He can hardly be likened to Job in his reaction to suffering. Whilst his attitude was mainly one of acceptance, there are hints that he was not without traces of protest in his character. One aspect of the life of Jesus that is not often emphasized is his occasional outbursts of anger. For example, John's gospel tells us that Jesus said, 'Take these things away; you shall not make my Father's house a house of trade' (2:16) when he saw all the buying and selling going on in the temple. He was a man of peace and yet he was at the same time a radical figure—he challenged people and stirred events up to the extent that he upset the authorities and was crucified as a criminal. He challenged traditional ideas of his time and disturbed the status quo. He questioned accepted norms, he showed anger and yet also vulnerability.

The gospels furnish us with little evidence of Jesus' attitude to suffering. We know that his whole ministry was one of healing, of relieving the suffering, of curing the blind and helping the lame to walk. He seems often to attribute suffering to demons opposed to God, as witnessed particularly in Mark's gospel. This is rather in keeping with the prologue of Job which can be said in a sense to exonerate God from some of the responsibility for suffering by bringing Satan into the picture. Suffering is seen sometimes to imply guilt and to be punishment for wrongdoing. For example, in the story of the healing of the paralytic man in Matthew 9:2 Jesus says, 'Take heart, my son; your sins are forgiven'. However, this is not true in every case and it is clearly not perceived as the fixed rule the friends of Job would have us believe. Rather than talk about the reasons for suffering, Jesus simply healed the sick and performed miracles, and then let others make what they would of the suffering which he knew to be his own ultimate destiny.

It is often overlooked that Jesus (like Job) suffered in his relationship with God. He knew God closely and yet he had moments of doubt (in the Garden of Gethsemane) and anguish (on the cross). He felt alone and forsaken by God, just as Job did. His suffering and his anguish did not lead to loss of belief—that would have denied who he was. But he went through the difficult process of acceptance all the same. He knew what God had in mind for him, that there was some plan and some purpose to his life, but this did not make his suffering any easier. He knew also that he had to suffer, that his suffering had a purpose and was on behalf of others. And yet somehow that knowledge did not lessen his suffering. He suffers real anguish. He prays in the Garden of Gethsemane: 'My Father, if it be possible, let this cup pass from me' (Matthew 26:42), and on the cross he cries, 'My God, my God, why hast thou forsaken me?' (Matthew 27:46).

Not only did Jesus suffer in his passion and crucifixion, but throughout his ministry, he was alive in an acute way to the evil around him. It has been said that the events of his passion indicate the lengths to which evil will go in its attempts to destroy goodness. Throughout his ministry he was spurned and rejected by others. Yet Jesus trusted in God absolutely and taught his followers to trust in him: 'Trust in God always, trust also in me'. In loving others, trust plays an important role—once that has gone from a relationship it can never be the same again. He gave other people the benefit of the doubt. Those whom others condemned as the down and outs of society he took notice of and spent time with.

Jesus promised that God will listen to prayer made in his name but did not promise that such action was a guarantee of reward nor that he could avert suffering as a result. Jesus spoke of a God of love who is there for us in our suffering, not of a magician who conjures up what we each want out of life. For Christians, forgiveness and freedom were won by Jesus on the cross—through him we can know that someone else is suffering with us and that we can make sense of it. We can also know that our sins are forgiven. Jesus conquered death by being raised from it, he showed it was not the end but a new beginning, and that by following his path some sense could be made out of life. There is no reward for good actions, but a knowledge of his presence with us, supporting us and comforting us—'I am with you always'—and giving us strength in our times of weakness. We might look at the piece by Canon Bezzant which I quoted at the beginning of this chapter. Particularly interesting in this context is his comment that 'the main purpose of religion...is not to give an intellectual answer to the most baffling of problems, but to give inner strength and power to gain the victory over the trials which provoke the questionings'.

For the Christian, as in the story of Job, there are two main reactions to suffering: either to accept what comes to us patiently and see the merits that a positive response to suffering can bring, or to protest in the face of injustice. The two responses are not incompatible as one can lead on to the other. Both have their place in Christian reflection and tradition. However, there is a sense in which the suffering of Jesus himself adds a more profound dimension to the problem of suffering. The world that crucified Jesus was one in which wickedness, misguidedness and self-interest won the day over goodness, holiness and love. In this it was much like our own world, with its self-seeking, materialistic attitudes, with its murderers and terrorists, with all that sickens and frightens us as we listen to the daily news. And yet in his suffering on the cross, Jesus took that evil and wickedness and suffering upon himself and showed that, far from it winning the day, God could overcome evil. Suffering is thus transformed and transcended by God by his presence in the midst of Christ's suffering. On the cross God enters into and bears the consequences of the existence of evil in the world that he has created. He shows his love for the created world, and so hope transcends the evil and the despair. Whatever suffering we may encounter, God is there.

A devotional response to the love of God in the suffering of Christ may thus be another answer—through prayer we may each be able to make some sense out of the suffering and maybe healing will finally come through acceptance. For the Christian there are no instant rewards, there is no point in holding up a very pious example. Like Jesus we are open to the precariousness of life and we have to trust in the love of God. Engaging in the suffering of others, being there to help when others need it, showing concern—these things are important. But at the heart of the Christian faith there is something more profound about the love of God and the hope that love inspires in the midst of the confusion of suffering. This is expressed well in Paul's second letter to the Corinthians (4:8–10): 'We are afflicted in every way, but not crushed; perplexed, but not driven to despair; persecuted, but not forsaken; struck down, but not destroyed; always carrying in the body the death of Jesus, so that the life of Jesus may also be manifested in our bodies'. This recalls the idea of the pushing out of limits I mentioned earlier in the book—just as you think you are at the end of your tether, some hidden strength often emerges from deep within the self. For Paul the thought of the crucified Christ was a source of this inner strength, which enabled him to go on with his mission and witness to others.

We might ask, finally, where does protest fit into this Christian response? Suffering often leads us to want to blame God, to vent our feelings. We have learned the legitimacy of such emotions from the biblical characters of protest, Job in particular, in the way they questioned God and his ways. If we are bold enough to do this—to stand up to God and question his ways—this might form a way of prayer which is almost entirely lacking in traditional spirituality. We are exhorted to adore

God, to praise him, to submit ourselves to his purposes. But much that goes on in the world makes us angry and there ought to be ways of expressing this in our prayers, not blaming God but trusting him in the midst of this anger. Protest is positive if it helps us to find a way of meeting suffering and moving on. Frances Young writes in an article on suffering, 'For many Christians, the book of Job voices their own protest, mystification, even blasphemy, in the face of innocent suffering; yet foreshadows the cross in that it points to the only acceptable response— that in God's presence all hurt and pain, all protests and questions cease and worship begins'. At the heart of Christianity is the understanding of God as love and, as we all know in our relationships with one another, love is given and not earned. We can try as hard as we like to win someone's love, but it is not to be bought or given on the accumulation of a certain number of credit points. Love is given freely by one person to another. So it is that God does not enable us to earn his love by making good things happen to us all the time, but rather he offers his love to us freely, through good and bad, through pain and anger and in all areas of our lives.

The traditional Christian answer to what our attitude should be to people who wrong us is that we should forgive them. This is easy enough to say but very hard to do. For example, if a brother or a son was killed in war, or by guerrilla warfare, would we not feel bitterness or hatred towards the nation or group who had inflicted the killing? To intercede on their behalf, to seek to atone for them, as Job eventually does for the friends, would be a way perhaps of meeting the bitterness and eventually overcoming it. Jesus said, 'Father forgive them, they know not what they do' (Luke 23:34). They need forgiveness, not just from us but also from God, and maybe one day they will come to accept that forgiveness. Looking outside ourselves to others is also a way of prayer. It is the final action we hear of Job doing before he is restored—his intercession for his friends. This is often a way of overcoming our own suffering or of preparing ourselves to overcome suffering if and when it comes in life. If our concern is only with ourselves we will find it hard to discover such a way.

I have quoted from Richard Harries' article 'Evidence for the love of God', and I find it interesting that, although he talks about suffering in the article, he has entitled it in this more positive way, putting the emphasis on a loving God rather than on suffering as a problem. In the end God has revealed to us his nature—he loves every one of us, he is here alongside us, and he is the last one that we should be blaming. He gave us freedom of choice out of his love for us, and that means that accidents happen, undeserved suffering occurs, and natural disasters too cannot be avoided. He created a world that works according to its own rules and gives us that stability of predictability that we need. God is love and he showed that love in the offering of his son Jesus Christ on the cross.

I want to end with a reminder of the words I quoted at the beginning of this chapter which come from MacLeish's play *JB*, and are the final words of Sarah, JB's wife: 'Blow on the coal of the heart'. The coal of the heart represents the burning ember of love left in a darkened world. These words come out of the darkness with the awareness that love is stronger than any other answer they have found. Even if God does not appear to love, human beings have an immense propensity to love. This suggests perhaps that God himself is the source of that love, and that rather than inflict suffering in an arbitrary way, he loves enough to suffer alongside us in a world which is full of unexplained calamity.

The Christian response is to point to God's love in offering the sacrifice of his son as atonement for the sins of humanity and as a sign of that love for humanity and the created world. He extends that love to every one of us as we seek to respond in love to Jesus and to follow in his way. Within that discipleship we have resources with which to face whatever suffering we meet and experience. A very proper part of that response to suffering is protest and questioning. Job metaphorically shook his fist at God and yet retained his faith in him—we should feel justified in doing the same.

Further Reading

In this list I will mention both books I have cited and other books or articles that may be of interest.

Books/articles on suffering:

Harries, R., 'Evidence for the love of God' in *Beyond Reasonable Doubt*, ed. G. Ryeland, Norwich, 1991

Kushner, H. S., *When bad things happen to good people*, London and Sydney, 1981

Lewis, C. S., *The Problem of Pain*, London, 1940

Longford, Lord, *Suffering and Hope*, London, 1990

Ten Boom, C., *The Hiding Place*, London, 1976

Wright, C. and Haines S., *Suffering: 'Why, silent God, why?'* Oxford, 1991

Young, F., 'Suffering' in *A New Dictionary of Christian Theology*, A. Richardson and J. Bowden (eds), London 1983, pp. 555–56

Fiction containing suffering amongst its themes:

Dostoyevsky, F., *The Brothers Karamazov*

Hardy, T., *The Mayor of Casterbridge*

Spark, M., *The Only Problem*

Other fiction cited:
Dahl, R., *Kiss Kiss*
Fowles, J., *The French Lieutenant's Woman*

Plays cited:
Becket, S., *Waiting for Godot,* 1956
MacLeish, A., *JB, A Play in Verse,* 1957
Shakespeare, W., *Hamlet*
Stoppard, T., *Rosencrantz and Guildenstern Are Dead,* 1967

Recommended books on Job:
Clines, D., *Job* (Word Biblical Commentary), Dallas, Texas, 1989
Dell, K. J., *The Book of Job As Sceptical Literature,* BZAW 197, Berlin and New York, 1991
Gordis, R., *The Book of God and Man,* Chicago, 1965
Mitchell, S., *The Book of Job,* San Francisco, 1987
Rowley, H. H., *Job* (New Century Bible Commentary), London and Grand Rapids, 1983

Books on protest literature:
Blank, S. H., 'Men against God: The Promethean Element in Biblical Prayer', JBL 72 (1953), pp. 1–13
Davidson, R. *The Courage to Doubt,* London, 1983
Crenshaw, J. L., *A Whirlpool of Torment,* Philadelphia, 1984
Vawter, B., *Job and Jonah: Questioning the Hidden God,* New Jersey, 1983
Campbell, A., *The Gospel of Anger,* London, 1986

Other works cited:
Crews, F., *The Pooh Perplex,* London, 1963
MacDonald, D. (ed.), *Parodies: an anthology from Chaucer to Beerbohm—and after,* London, 1960
The Holocaust, guide from Yad Vashem, Jerusalem

Acknowledgements

Unless otherwise stated, all biblical references are from the Revised Standard Version of the Bible, © 1952, 1971, 1976 Division of Christian Education of the National Council of the Churches of Christ, USA.

Throughout there are quotations from the play, *JB*, by Archibald MacLeish, used by permission of his Estate and the William Morris Agency, New York.

About the Author

D r Katharine Dell studied Theology at St Hugh's College, Oxford, and earned a D. Phil in Old Testament at Oriel College, Oxford. She has lectured in the Old Testament at Ripon College, Cuddesdon, and at St John's and Mansfield Colleges, Oxford. She is currently a Fellow of St Catharine's College, Cambridge, where she directs Theology and Religious Studies. Her special area of interest is the wisdom literature of the Old Testament, and she is Secretary of the Society for Old Testament Study. She is the author of *The Book of Job As Sceptical Literature*.